The Complete Book

FLY CASTING

by JOHN ALDEN KNIGHT
and RICHARD ALDEN KNIGHT

FLY casting is a sport engaged in by millions of anglers—the number increases each year—but it is an intricate sport, requiring concentrated effort and practice. This book —the next best thing to a series of personal lessons by two renowned experts—covers every aspect of the science and art of fly casting—from the basic rudiments through all the advanced refinements.

Detailed information is provided on fly-rod equipment, the fundamentals of the sport, wet-fly casting, dry-fly casting, line handling, bass-bug casting, salt-water fly casting, special casts for special fishing situations, lengthening the cast. In addition, new, remarkably effective techniques (devised by the authors) such as the "free-wrist grip" and the "floating elbow"—techniques described nowhere else — are prominently featured.

Thorough and authoritative, this is a complete illustrated manual that will not only enable the amateur who has never before cast a fly to become, with a little practice, a proficient fly caster, but will also serve to increase the skill and enjoyment of the experienced fisherman.

The Complete Book of FLY CASTING

JOHN ALDEN KNIGHT

The

of

and RICHARD ALDEN KNIGHT

Complete Book
FLY CASTING

PHOTOGRAPHS BY PODY

G. P. Putnam's Sons　New York

TO OUR GIRLS—MAMA AND JAC

CONTENTS

THE AUTHORS

JOHN ALDEN KNIGHT and RICHARD ALDEN KNIGHT are the only father and son team in the Fishing Hall of Fame. The senior author is widely known as the publisher of the Solunar Tables, which lists the feeding and activity periods of fish and game for each day of the year in all parts of the country, and as the writer of a syndicated column on fishing and shooting which appears in over 140 newspapers in the United States and Canada. In addition to numerous magazine articles, he has written *The Modern Angler, The Theory and Technique of Fresh-Water Angling, Field Book of Fresh-Water Angling* and ten other books. He has also been the first man to conduct a lecture course on angling as a member of the Columbia University faculty. Richard Alden Knight has written many articles on fishing and hunting for such publications as *Field and Stream, Outdoor Life* and *Sports Illustrated*. He holds a number of fly-casting records. Both authors live in Williamsport, Pennsylvania.

WHEN I heard that the fishing Knights were working on a book together, I couldn't help but chuckle to myself. If ever two strong-minded men were to be picked as completely unlikely to succeed in a collaboration, the Knights would have to be my choice. It had to be a fight to the finish. Look at the record.

The elder author, Jack Knight, likes to fish for bonefish; his son Dick can't tolerate the beasties. Junior will spend hours digging through heavy water in a trout stream with a nymph after lunker browns, while Senior will wait for a hatch. When it comes to rods and design, they are in constant warfare as to which is best. I have watched Junior battle tarpon far larger than the tackle could handle and lose them happily; Senior shakes his head. One thing does stand out, however—these two men have learned more about the fly rod than any other two men in the world.

I first met Dick Knight when he was Tournament Director of the International Tarpon Tournament in 1961. He is a stocky, well-built man, his personality reflecting his love of the outdoors. In his thirty-eight years he has made a name for himself in the field of fishing that is hard to top, and I was pleased to induct him into the Fishing Hall of Fame as its youngest member.

During my stay at the tournament I watched Junior in action, fishing before the cameras of a major movie crew. His job—to jump and catch tarpon. His score—78 fish hooked, jumped and landed in eight days! He did it all, so help me, on 30-pound conventional tackle! Watching him corral a big fish, whittle him down to size, teach him to jump on cue for a camera and then land him when requested, was a sight I won't forget for a long time.

Dick started casting when he was two and a half years old and has been doing it ever since. His record with a fly is impressive—he still holds the fly-rod championship on shark since landing a 136-pounder on standard gear. The last time I heard from him he was working on white marlin off Long Island, attempting the improbable feat of taking one of these bombers on a salt-water fly rod.

Dick has powerful casting form, while still maintaining the grace that has made this act a thing of beauty to watch. He leans toward the parabolic rod tapers, preferring to drive a line rather than float it to a target. His accuracy is as deadly as his ability, once a fish is hooked.

I have been corresponding with the senior author of this book for at least thirty years, but our first meeting was at the International Tarpon Tournament held at Punta Gorda, Florida, in 1961. While there we spent two days together in Charley Wheeler's cruiser, *Miss Betty*, drifting the famous pass at Boca Grande, Florida. Admittedly, we did more talking than fishing during those two days, going over the happenings of past years.

Jack is a big fellow—6 feet 1 and 192 pounds. He is not a voluble man, and he talks only when he has something to say. Moreover, he is a good listener. You've heard tell of dedicated men? Well, this man is exactly that. He is a clear thinker and quite resourceful, with the result that he has piled up a record that stands by itself in angling history. Let's take a look at the high spots of that record.

He is a college graduate, Cornell, 1915, where he took an A. B. Law degree. He started serious writing back in 1932 when he introduced the artificial nymph to the angling public. This is his twelfth published book, many of them standard works on their subjects. How many magazine articles he has written over the years is anybody's guess. He handles a shotgun just about as well as he does a fly rod. He has a list of "firsts" that is truly impressive. Here are some of the more important ones:

Originator of the Barometric Theory and its effect on wildlife—1928.

Originator of the Solunar Theory—1926.

First published the *Solunar Tables*—1935. (Incidentally, the *Solunar Tables* are now published in eleven foreign editions throughout the globe, in seven foreign languages.)

Originator of nymph fishing in this country (he tied the first flat-bodied nymphs)—1933.

Creator of several fly patterns, the best known being the Knighthawk and the Mickey Finn.

With Charles Ritz of Paris, introduced the parabolic rod action which has had much influence on modern rod design.

In *Modern Fly Casting*, introduced the free-wrist grip with accent on the high back cast which did much to alter tournament casting styles.

Was experimenting with bass bugs way back in 1919, about the same time as Call McCarthy and Will Dilg.

Was first to conduct a university lecture course on angling, as a member of Columbia University faculty—1938–40.

First to write a nationally syndicated column on the outdoors—1947. (Now published in 140 newspapers in the United States and Canada.)

First outdoor writer to receive the gold plaque of the original Hunting and Fishing Hall of Fame.

First outdoor writer to receive the Dolphin Award of the Fishing Hall of Fame.

First President of the Sportsman's Club International.

Incidentally, Jack and Dick constitute the only father-and-son combination in the Fishing Hall of Fame.

As stated earlier, the possibility of a successful collaboration between this hardheaded pair seemed doubtful. But they managed to get it done and done well. Too bad I couldn't be on hand to listen to some of the arguments.

In the pages of this book, these two men have made a definite contribution to the sport of angling. Until now, there has been no complete book of fly casting. There was a need for one and now we have it. I know the two authors well and you have my assurance that you can believe what they tell you.

The Complete Book of FLY CASTING

Plate 1. Richard Alden Knight and John Alden Knight.

HISTORY OF THE FLY ROD 1

I T would be exceedingly difficult to state accurately just when the idea of the fly rod first came to the mind of man. As far back as 2000 B.C., the Macedonians were using artificial flies to take fish from the Nile. How the fly was presented to the fish is not stated in ancient writings, but it must have been done by using a fly rod of some kind. More than 3,000 years later, in the year 1500, we learn of the angling activities of Dame Juliana Berners, prioress of Sopwell Nunnery in Great Britain. Dame Juliana tied her own flies and has left a list of her series of twelve patterns, one for each month of the year. Surely she must have used some form of fly rod to present these flies to the fish, although, unfortunately, she has little to say about tackle in her writings.

The Days of Cotton and Walton

Izaak Walton and his friend Charles Cotton have all too little to say about rods in their "discourses." Evidently they did not completely agree on rods. For example, Walton, in his admonitions to Venator, cautions: "First, let your rod be light and gentle; I take the best to be of two pieces." Conversely, Cotton says about rods: ". . . of these, the best that ever I saw are made in Yorkshire: which are all of one piece, that is to say of several, six, eight, ten or twelve pieces, so neatly pieced and tied together with fine thread below and silk above as to make it taper like a switch, and to ply with a true bent in your hand. And these, too, are light, being made of firwood for two or three lengths nearest to the hand, and of other wood nearer to the top, that a man might, very easily, manage the longest of them that I ever saw, with one hand." Incidentally, Cotton suggests that these rods be taken down for winter storage, the sections oil-dressed and "layed flat." Imagine, if you can, the chore of getting such a rod reassembled and ready for spring fishing.

Antique Construction

As time went on, fly-rod construction became more or less standardized. Lancewood, bethabara, and greenheart came to be recognized as the best fly-rod materials. Since lancewood is somewhat lighter than the other two woods, some rodmakers built fly rods in three pieces, the two lower sections being made of bethabara or greenheart and the upper or tip section of lancewood. However, the great majority of the earlier fly rods were, as Walton suggested, of two-piece construction. This is quite understandable when one considers that until comparatively recent years ferrules were not used to join rod sections together. Instead, the ends were beveled, the angles being carefully cut so that the rods would be straight, and then the beveled sections were bound firmly in place with stout cord reinforced with a dressing of resin or beeswax to prevent slipping. This manner of juncture had an advantage, as the flexibility of the rod was not impaired by the insertion of a short section of comparatively inflexible metal. The old wooden rods were heavy compared with modern rods, but they had a quality about them that modern anglers have not experienced. Indeed, English writings contain frequent references to the "sweetness of greenheart."

In 1929, an angler fishing the east branch of the Delaware River of New York State was using one of these old greenheart rods, bound with friction tape at the juncture of the two pieces. He was an Irishman, newly come to this country, and in his youth he had been a salmon gillie on Ireland's famous Blackwater. The rod was a huge affair, designed for two-handed casting. The action was slow but obviously powerful, and for the task then in hand—fishing minnows in a big trout river—it was ideally suited to the purpose. The owner said that he preferred it to any of the modern fly rods.

But rods made of wood had one serious defect that was impossible to eliminate—all of them would warp. In the United States, some of the rodmakers tried local woods in rod construction, mostly hickory and ash. When new, these rods performed every bit as well as those made of imported woods, but despite all the care that could be given them, they would warp to the point of uselessness. Thus it is understandable that anglers and rodmakers were not completely satisfied with rods made of wood.

The Development of Bamboo

Since the search for new and better materials for rod building went on constantly, it was almost inevitable that bamboo—the material for which Orientals have a thousand uses—be employed in fly-rod construction. Bamboo is not actually a wood in the sense that a tree is a wood. It is one of the grasses, and unlike wood, the grain is usually straight; thus, bamboo cane lends itself to splitting quite well.

The ease with which bamboo can be split into uniform, hard, narrow strips makes it useful in producing such things as baskets, mats, chair seats, furniture, etc. The whole cane, being extremely light in relation to its strength, is used in building houses, small bridges, ships' masts and so on, while smaller sections are made into flutes, pipe stems and walking sticks, to name only a few. Indeed, the word "cane" has come to replace "walking stick" in our vocabulary.

In the early eighteen hundreds, Americans were far too busy consolidating their new-found independence and carving out fresh territory in the wilderness to concern themselves much about fly rods. After all, fish in those days represented food for hungry families. An alder pole, a homemade line and hook baited with whatever was handy, would provide all the fish that was needed. Most people simply did not have the time to devote to sport fishing.

This was not so in Great Britain, however. In 1847, Edward Fitzgibbon, of London, published his *Handbook of Angling*. In it he quotes a Mr. Little of No. 15 Fetter Lane, London, rodmaker to His Royal Highness Prince Albert, speaking of the top and middle joints of a salmon rod:

They [the two rod joints] are to be made from the stoutest pieces of bamboo cane, called "jungle," and brought from India. The pieces should be large and straight, so that you can rend them well through the knots and all. Each joint should consist of three rent pieces . . . and afterward glued together, knot opposite to knot . . . but the best part opposite to that which may be imperfect, so as to equalize defectiveness and goodness. The natural badness of the cane you counteract by art, and none save a clever workman can do it.

Mr. Fitzgibbon then adds his own comment: "In my opinion, rods . . . made entirely of rent and glued jungle-cane are the best. They must be most carefully fashioned, and no maker can turn them out without charging a high price. I am also of the opinion that they will last longer than any other sort of rod, and are far less liable to warping."

After bestowing his blessing, in no uncertain terms, on the desirability of split-cane rods, it is interesting to note what he had to say in the next edition of his book, published a year later in 1848. "I have changed my opinion with respect to rods made entirely of rent cane or any other wood rent. Their defects will always more than counter-balance their merits."

Fitzgibbon says in his first book that a Mr. Bowness, another London tacklemaker, had shown him a rent-cane rod "that had been for many years in use and was still as straight as a wand." Applying a reasonable interpretation to the words "for many years," the probabilities are that British rodmakers were experimenting with split-cane rods as early as 1830 and certainly no later than 1840.

In 1851, at the Crystal Palace Exhibition in London, Mr. Thomas Aldred, of London, showed a split-cane rod and (Fitzgibbon, Little, Bowness, *et al.*, to the contrary notwithstanding) claimed to be the inventor of the rod built entirely of rent cane. This was a three-strip affair, rounded rather than three-sided. Of course, it was not surprising that Fitzgibbon changed his opinion of rent-cane rods when you consider that much of the hard outside bark or enamel was removed when the three-strip rod section was rounded.

The Phillipi Rod Leads the Way

But the first approach to a really good, common-sense bamboo fly rod must be credited to Sam Phillipi, a gunmaker of Easton, Pennsylvania, in 1862. Evidently realizing the shortcomings of the split-bamboo rods that had been turned out up to that time, he made a six-strip fly rod of Calcutta cane. So far as we know, he made only three of these rods. One is now on display in the clubroom of the Anglers Club of New York. The other two are still in the possession of Phillipi's family.

Naturally, the Phillipi rod has been examined with a great deal of interest. It is a three-piece affair, about 9 feet long and weighing about 6 ounces. The action is somewhat faster than might be expected, mostly confined to the upper half of the rod. Actually, by modern standards, it is only a fair fly rod, but it served to point the way to the manufacture of better rods.

On January 23, 1831, there was born at Sebec, Piscataquis County, Maine, a man who has left a firm and lasting imprint on the history of rodmaking and on the entire rodmaking industry, Hiram Lewis Leonard. His family traveled, moving to Ellenville, New York, some years later to Honesdale, Pennsylvania, and later to Bangor, Maine. Leonard worked as a gunsmith and a taxidermist and in 1871 made his first fishing rod. This rod, built for his own personal use, was made of ash and lancewood. Leonard had inspected some rods made by Tom Conway of New York and felt that he could make a better one. The rod so impressed those who saw it that he was persuaded to show it to Bradford & Anthony, a sporting-goods house in Boston.

As a result, Bradford & Anthony, which had not been too happy about its fishing rods—particularly those of bamboo—had one of its salesmen take two samples to show to

Leonard. These were bamboo rods of the 4-strip variety, and Leonard told the salesman that he could make better ones. Recognizing at once the faulty engineering in these samples, he made his first bamboo rods with sections of 6 strips. This was in 1871. The rods were a great success, and Bradford & Anthony sent in orders for more and more. Business boomed and Leonard found it necessary to hire help in his shop.

It was not long before Leonard broke off relations with Bradford & Anthony and marketed his rods through the old New York jobbinghouse of Abbey & Imbrie. About that time, 1877, he went into partnership with a Boston man named Kidder. A year later Kidder sold his interest in the H. L. Leonard Rod Company to the famous tacklehouse, William Mills & Son of New York City. The "son," incidentally, was Thomas B. Mills.

Mills found that the location of the Leonard factory in Bangor, Maine, was quite inconvenient and persuaded Leonard to move his plant to Central Valley, New York, where it is today. Leonard brought with him from Maine four rodmakers, W. Edwards, E. F. Payne, F. E. Thomas and Hiram Hawes. This group was soon augmented by Loman Hawes (Hiram's brother) and Frank Oram. In time, six of Leonard's rodmakers—Thomas, Payne, Chubb, Devine, Edwards and Hawes—left the Leonard plant to start factories of their own, all producing high-grade bamboo rods. The fame of Leonard rods soon spread throughout the United States and then to England. They won first prizes at exhibitions in Vienna and London as well as at the World's Fair in Philadelphia.

Strangely enough, the earlier rodmakers did not agree on the universal use of ferrules on their rods. Some of them who were turning out rods in the early nineteen hundreds still used the beveled juncture of the joints, which had to be bound together with wrappings of stout cord, these rods being made of greenheart, bethabara and lancewood as well as bamboo. Not until the invention of the shouldered, waterproofed ferrule, serrated where metal met wood, was the beveled juncture finally discarded.

The Use of Tonkin Cane

Calcutta cane, of which most of the earlier split-cane rods were made, has its greatest strength in the outside bark or skin. Once this is removed, the life of the cane is gone. For this reason, the action of a fly rod had to be designed and built into the rod when the strips were planed, prior to gluing. Conversely, the rodmakers soon learned that Tonkin cane (butt-cut stalks of which are taken from the windy, seaward slopes of what used to be the Tonkin Province of French Indochina) is a tough, resilient bamboo on which the outer skin is of no value. This cane lends itself to "benchwork." In other words, the action of a fly rod can be shaped *after* the rod sections have been glued up and assembled. Planing-in the desired action was done, for the most part, with "sand blocks"—blocks of wood over which fine sandpaper had been stretched. When one considers that the flexibility of a fly rod varies as the *cube* of the diameter, it can readily be seen that sanding or planing the proper action into a rod section can be an extremely technical job. Only top-grade rodmakers were equal to the task, and it is this unseen workmanship which elevates the price of a high-grade bamboo fly rod.

Down through the years much experimentation has been done in the assembly of split-bamboo rod sections. Soon after the use of Tonkin cane became general, rod sections once again were planed off round. From an engineering standpoint, the round rod section is the soundest, as this construction provides the longest diameter for the size of the section. Since any flexible bar or rod will bend at right angles to the *shortest* diameter, the round section gives the greatest efficiency for the amount of the wood used in that section.

As stated earlier, the British rodmakers used the method of rounding their three-strip sections, but the loss of most of the vital outside shell on those Calcutta strips defeated their purpose. Since then, rods have been built with four-strip, five-strip and six-strip sections. About 1912, the firm of Abbey & Imbrie had on the market a fly rod with the name "steel vine." This was a three-section rod, the sections perfectly round, built of Tonkin cane. The four-strip, with the 90-degree strips, obviously is bad engineering. Some companies still glue up five-strip sections, the theory being that the high point of wood opposite the guides adds power to the rod. This is true up to a point; the trouble is that the flexing rod seeks that shorter diameter, causing a five-strip rod to cast off-line.

The great majority of the companies which manufacture split-bamboo rods now make them in six-strip or hexagonal sections. After these have been glued and dried, the sharp edges at the junctions of the strips are planed off, as is the useless outer skin of the Tonkin cane. This results in a rod section which is partially rounded, and these rods have functioned quite satisfactorily for many years.

Taper Development

The earlier fly rods were given uniform or "circular" taper. It was soon learned, however, that the uniform taper, while good, was not all that might be desired. With the uniform taper, at the completion of a forward cast, the rod tip follows through with a decided dip, making the throwing of a straight line rather difficult. Thus, the parabolic taper was evolved. This was the result of a collaboration between Charles Ritz, of Paris, France, and the senior author of this book. Jim Payne, of the Payne Rod Company, made for us the first parabolic fly rod, a 7-foot, 9-inch affair. With it, it was possible to throw a perfectly straight line, since there was no follow-through of the tip at the completion of the forward cast. In Charles Ritz's book, *A La Mouche*, there is the reproduction of a photograph of this rod, taken in the Beaverkill River in New York State, throwing a measured cast of 78 feet, at the completion of which the 9-foot leader and fly "turned over" so that the fly alighted on the water before the leader and line. But the true parabolic rod left much to be desired. It was a clubby affair which required absolute perfection in timing, a gift which, lamentably, the average fly caster does not have. Regretfully, the notion of putting the true parabolic action into production was discarded.

Meanwhile, Edward Ringwood Hewitt came up with his short-lived "steep taper" rod action. This rod was turned out for a short while at the Leonard factory of William Mills & Son. Most of the action of the steep taper is confined to the upper third of the rod. For fishing small streams with a short line, it is a fairly usable rod; but for use in a big trout river where casts of more than 40 feet are the order of the day, it is an abomination. It is not, and never was, a very good rod, although the soft tip does lend itself to the sure hooking of a rising trout.

During the development of split bamboo as a rod material, another material began to appear in rod construction—steel. Steel rods were being manufactured as early as 1900, but the inherent characteristics of steel were against it from the start. The weight-to-resiliency or -elasticity ratio was completely out of balance when compared to bamboo. True, a great many steel rods were sold and used down through the years. One company actually succeeded in working out a method for satisfactory tapering—although this deviated from the usual uniform taper—but the rods themselves, at their very best, never were in the same class with split bamboo. Then, with the advent of glass as a rod material, steel was almost entirely discarded. Today you will have difficulty finding a steel fly rod in any of the sporting-goods stores.

The Semiparabolic

Meanwhile, rod design, as it was in 1936, was soon to undergo a rather radical change for the better. In Yonkers, New York, Dr. George Parker Holden had taken under his wing, so to speak, a young man named Everett Garrison. The late Dr. Holden is the author of two delightful books—*The Idyl of the Split Bamboo* and *Streamcraft*. For a great many years, fishing had been his absorbing hobby, and more particularly he was passionately devoted to rodmaking. Dr. Holden split his own cane, planed his own strips, and glued up his own rod sections. No factory-made, glued-up rod sections for him. He was a forceful character, sufficient unto himself. When Everett Garrison came to him with a request to learn the art of rod building, Dr. Holden set out to teach him all that he could.

Garrison is what can only be described properly as a "natural mechanic"; he was born with mechanic's hands wherein precision was a built-in factor. Holden recognized this gift and he gave Garrison the benefit of his years of experience. Garrison soon set up a small shop in his own home and started making split-bamboo rods in 1933.

One day in the spring of 1937, Garrison showed up at the clubrooms of the Anglers Club of New York with seven rod cases under his arm. After lunch, he took the rods from their cases and laid them out side by side on the library table. Three of these rods were quite good, excellent in fact. The other four were only so-so.

In the course of the conversation around the library table that day, the matter of the parabolic action in a fly rod was discussed. Actually, this type of rod action had not at that time been given the name "parabolic." That came later, the following year. However, the idea of this new wrinkle in rod action was impressed on Garrison, and his engineering mind caught the theory quickly.

Over the course of the next two months, Garrison built eight rods in the attempt to incorporate the parabolic principle into fly-rod action. The first of this series was not a good rod; in fact, it was a very bad one. An hour's casting on the lawn revealed most of the "bugs," and he tried again. Gradually the rods became better. The eighth was, and still is, a dream rod which has been in active use for more than 25 years. This rod is 8 feet long and weighs slightly less than 4 ounces; it is of 2-piece construction. In its action, Garrison had at long last found the answer to the problem of incorporating the parabolic principle in a rod that any fly caster could use. For want of a better term, it was called the "semiparabolic" rod action.

It did not take long for Garrison's semiparabolic rod action to make itself felt throughout the industry. Briefly, the parabolic idea is this: instead of having the action distributed more or less evenly throughout the entire rod, the parabolic action proper—the actual bending—is confined pretty much to the lower one third of the rod. The center one third bends comparatively little, acting much like a lever. The top one third does have some tip action for the final imparting of the force of the cast to the line, while the top 8 or 10 inches are tapered rather abruptly to provide a soft tip and thus insure reasonably sure hooking. This general idea was incorporated into the semi-parabolic action, modifying it so that the rod did not place such a high premium on perfect timing. The general idea showed up quickly enough in the rods of the majority of the companies, even being quite noticeable in plug-casting rods and spinning rods. Actually, this action does make a great deal of sense, as it endows a rod of fairly light weight with a disproportionate amount of power for its size, a particularly useful quality when applied to dry-fly fishing, in which a great deal of "false casting" is a necessity.

Plastics and Resins

In the nineteen thirties, a veritable flood of plastics was developed. Before that time, Bakelite was the outstanding plastic in general commercial use. But when the resin plastics, the polyesters and Du Pont's nylon came out, certain anglers and rodmakers began to experiment. At the Bakelight factory it was learned that bamboo could be completely impregnated with this material, thereby rendering the rod section waterproof and in no need of a protective coat of spar varnish. These rods are being made today by the Charles F. Orvis Company, and they stand the test of time very well indeed.

Edward Ringwood Hewitt almost came up with the ideal solution to the problem of finding good rod material. In a wooden form or mold, he stretched lengthwise hundreds of fine strands of nylon. These were cemented together with one of the then newer plastics. The result was a round rod section of uniform taper. However, nylon proved to be too elastic for the job and it allowed more bending than the plastic could stand. With a little use, the rod section soon would being to disintegrate.

The Use of Glass

In June 1944, Dr. Arthur M. Howald, of Libby-Owens Ford Glass Company, was indulging in his favorite pastime, trout fishing. He hooked an exceptionally large trout and in the course of the battle managed to break a rod tip. At that time (during World War II) bamboo rod tips were exceedingly difficult to obtain. Dr. Howald decided to build a rod tip to replace the broken one.

As Technical Director of the Plaskan Division of Libby-Owens Ford, he was familiar with glass fibers and plastics. First he constructed a mold the size and taper of the broken rod tip. Next, using a strip of soft wood as a mandrel or core, he laid in glass fibers and then cemented the fibers and wooden core together with a resin plastic. The result was a fiberglass rod tip that functioned quite well.

This novel method of using fiberglass as a rod material was shown to the Shakespeare Company of Kalamazoo, Michigan, which undertook several years of experimentation. In 1947, the Shakespeare Company had fiberglass rods on display at the annual Sportsmen's Show in New York, then held at the Grand Central Palace on Lexington Avenue.

As might be expected, the rods were not what might be called top grade. But they had many advantages not characteristic of bamboo rods. First and foremost, glass rods need little or no care. They are waterproof and weatherproof. Only the guide windings need varnish now and then. Moreover, they do not warp. These facts were quite strongly brought out by Vernon "Gadabout" Gaddis, the Shakespeare representative then in charge of the display booth. When the taper and action of the rods were commented on with the suggestion that there was considerable room for improvement, Gaddis replied that the factory was so far behind in filling orders that the facilities could not begin to keep up with the demand. Time enough to worry about improved taper and action when the boys at the factory had a chance to catch their collective breath.

These original fiberglass rods were of the "solid glass" variety. The wooden core, as used by Dr. Howald in that first glass rod tip, had been discontinued. Instead, the rods were of solid construction, glass fibers and plastic. It was not long, however, before tubular construction was introduced. The Conolan Corporation, of Costa Mesa, California, a subsidiary of the Garcia Corporation, is credited with putting the first tubular rod sections on the market. Shakespeare soon followed suit, as did Heddon and others.

It must be remembered that manufacturing processes in the rodmaking industry are not by any means public property. Actually, the details of manufacture are carefully guarded and it is not the usual thing to allow visitors to go through the factories and inspect procedures. This has been true ever since the introduction of split-bamboo rod sections. This secrecy concerning manufacturing details is particularly true today in the glass-rod industry. Fabricating methods are new and the details are closely guarded. However, the factories have been generous in supplying enough information so that generalization is possible.

Fiberglass Construction

The Shakespeare Company holds the basic patents on glass-rod construction in so far as the method of laying longitudinal glass fibers in a mold is concerned. This is

THE MANUFACTURE OF A TUBULAR GLASS ROD

Plate 2. V-shaped cut is made, depending on the rod's length and action. This cut can be varied to place action anywhere in the rod, and the butt can be made stronger or weaker, according to the needs of the fisherman.

Plate 3. The glass cloth pattern is heat-sealed to a steel mandrel, or tapered rod, and is then rolled around this rod. At this point the material is "tacky" and adheres to itself until the next operation can be performed.

Plate 4. Cellophane tape is wound around the rod to place the cloth under tension while it is properly cured or heat-treated.

Plate 5. Preparatory to curing, the rods are fixed in hanging racks. These racks are hung to the slow-moving conveyor which takes them to a thermostatically controlled oven.

Plate 6. Rods have now completed curing, and are being taken from the oven where they will be sent through a cellophane removal operation, and the steel mandrels will be withdrawn.

Plate 7. Each tubular section is now given a careful final inspection as they are gauged, marked to show where metal fittings and guides are to be placed, and sent on to final finishing operations.

Plate 8. After various component parts such as ferrules, handles, etc., have been added, the rod then goes to winding where the guides and colorful trim are put on by skillful workers.

true both for rods of "solid glass" and of tubular construction. But the other companies soon hit upon another construction method—wrapping finely woven glass cloth around a mandrel—which, evidently, is outside the claims of the original patent. To be sure, in the glass-cloth method only the longitudinal fibers are working, the lateral fibers merely taking up space, but the rods turned out by this method are surprisingly good. It is a moot question as to which method produces the better rods.

Actually, during the past five years or so, glass has almost come to replace bamboo as a rod material. If you go into the average sporting-goods store today, the probabilities are that you will find no bamboo rods in the display rack. This does not mean, however, that high-grade bamboo rods are no longer available. In the top-notch tackleshops, bamboo rods are still to be found, but the prices are much, much higher than the prevailing prices of glass rods. The reason for this variance in price is quite obvious. Rods of good Tonkin cane are assembled by trained, experienced rodmakers. There is much extra labor involved in a bamboo rod when compared with a glass rod which, by the very nature of its construction, must be classed as a "production job."

Whether or not bamboo will disappear completely as a rod material is anybody's guess. Surely it *has* disappeared in rods of the medium-price class. Of course, there are the bamboo rods of Japanese manufacture carried by some of the stores, but these are cheap affairs, actually not worth the little that is paid for them. Then, too, it must be remembered that the source of good butt-cut Tonkin cane is now in Communist hands and little or no cane is being imported. This may make a difference in the availability of bamboo rods in future years. But the American companies are making rapid strides in the improvement of the casting quality of glass rods. Tapers, too, are being improved. Only time can provide the answer concerning the ultimate rod material.

SELECTING A FLY ROD | 2

THERE is no such thing as an all-purpose fly rod. A rod that is good for a certain kind of fishing is just about useless on other waters. Time was when many fly fishermen went so far as to differentiate between trout fly rods, dividing them into wet-fly rods and dry-fly rods. Since the introduction of the semiparabolic taper, however, a good trout rod—a really good one—will handle both dry flies and wet flies very well indeed. There is no need to carry a slow rod and a fast rod nowadays; the semiparabolic taper will take care of just about any task you set for it on a trout stream.

But there are many kinds of fishing these days to which the fly rod has been adapted. Originally, the fly rod was intended to cast flies on a trout stream. Then its scope was widened to include salmon fishing, but it was still meant to cast flies—imitations of the natural stream insects. Hence its name—fly rod. But today the lures that are cast with fly rods frequently bear little resemblance to stream insects; witness the bass bug, and hair beetle and hair frog, and the bucktails and streamer flies which are supposed to represent or "suggest" small fish or minnows.

The result is that fly-rod design is just as diversified as the uses to which a fly rod is put: trout fishing, bass fishing, salmon fishing, and even salt-water fishing. In this last category, rods are divided into two classes—bonefish rods and heavy-duty or "flat" rods for such fish as tarpon, snook, jack crevalle, etc. However, there are some generalities that apply to *all* fly rods. Let's examine these first.

While the vast majority of rods sold today are made of glass, there are many die-hards among the fly fishermen who insist that there is nothing in glass that can compare with the ideal casting quality of good bamboo. Thus, they are willing to lay out the extra cash needed to purchase a good bamboo rod. Conversely, the average angler is quite happy with glass, particularly tubular glass. To be sure, most of these fellows have never had the opportunity to fish with a high-grade Tonkin-cane fly rod. As a matter of fact, not very many of the younger fly fishermen of today have so much as *seen* such a rod, much less fished with one.

Perhaps the best way to form a comparison is to list both the advantages and the disadvantages of the two types.

Bamboo—Pro and Con

In the first place, bamboo rods are, after all, made of wood (cellulose, wood fiber, call it what you will); and wood, as we all know, is affected by several things—oxidation, temperature, mildew, overwork or overstrain which tires the fibers, and, most important, moisture. The strips of a bamboo rod section are held together with animal glue, usually the casein variety. Glue, almost any kind of glue, is easily affected by moisture or mildew, and this is particularly true of animal glue. Thus, if you store your rod in a closed container that may hold even a trace of moisture, your rod section will come apart.

Sometimes there are sections between the strips which have not been glued quite as well as the rest of the rod. When subjected to severe strain, these sections tend to slip and the rod will take a "set" or, in other words, bend slightly out of line.

Bamboo rods are protected from the atmosphere by several coats of waterproof varnish. The trouble is that there is no such thing as a completely nonporous varnish. The varnish of a rod left out all night, so that it becomes covered with dew, is almost always penetrated by some of this moisture in certain places. To be sure, the rod can be dried out so that little damage results, but over the years moisture does take its toll.

Temperature, particularly heat, can damage a bamboo rod. In the factories, rod sections are straightened by the application of mild heat and subsequent flexing. Allow a bamboo rod to become hot by, for example, laying it on top of an automobile which is standing in the sun; then subject it to a sudden strain and the rod will take a set.

Wood fibers do become tired after continued use, and an old bamboo rod which has been to the wars is apt to lose much of its original life. There is nothing to do in this event but buy another rod.

Offsetting these drawbacks, however, is the superb casting quality of good bamboo. There is nothing quite like it so far in glass. And that's what the bamboo addicts pay for when they buy a high-grade rod.

Glass—Pro and Con

Glass has many advantages that bamboo definitely does not have. As mentioned earlier, moisture does not affect

Plate 9. A battery of fine rods. *Left to right:* salt-water "flat rod," 9 feet;
Winston dry-fly rod, 8½ feet; Winston dry-fly rod, 8 feet; Pizon and Michel
Parabolic, 7 feet 9 inches; Orvis impregnated, 6½ feet; Abercrombie & Fitch
fly-rod baby, 44 inches; Leonard grilse rod, 9 feet 10 inches; Leonard
"Knight 99"; Winston salt-water bonefish rod, 9½ feet.

glass. You can store a glass rod in a damp case and nothing will happen to the rod proper. To be sure, varnish on the guide windings may show the effects of damp storage, but not the rod itself. And heat will not affect a glass rod. By heat is meant, usually, the sort of heat that a rod would encounter in ordinary use: a hot car top, for example, or standing too long in the midday sun. Oxidation and mildew do not affect glass. Continued use does weary glass fibers to some extent, but not as much as it does bamboo fibers. About the only way you can damage a glass rod is to rap it sharply against some hard object; dropping one on a rocky beach will do it. After all, it *is* glass and it will shatter or chip, even though held together by resin plastic.

Added to the foregoing advantages are two more important characteristics. Glass is infinitely stronger than bamboo, and, ounce-for-ounce, packs more resiliency and casting power.

To illustrate, one day a man was fishing in upper Florida Bay. Admittedly, this man was not an expert fisherman. He did things with tackle that an experienced angler wouldn't dream of doing. That day he was fishing for redfish and snook in fairly shallow water. He had cast to a feeding redfish. The cast proved to be too long, and instead of shortening line by stripping it in through the guides, he raised the tip of the rod to bring the fly within the field of vision of the feeding fish.

Suddenly out of the deeper water beyond the redfish came a fairly large jack crevalle. The jack took the fly in full stride. As the angler attempted to set the hook, the jack, feeling the tension, darted to the left. Then, just as rapidly, he darted to the right. The rod was pulled down over the man's right shoulder, across his back, and then

Plate 10. Pioneers in glass construction. Henry Shakespeare (left) and William Shakespeare, Jr., demonstrating the near-unbreakable qualities of one of their earliest rods. Constructed of solid glass, this rod was the forerunner of the present-day models.

around his waist where it stayed while the jack went away against the tension of the reel. A bamboo rod would have been ruined completely by such treatment, but the glass rod, which he had borrowed, not only stood up under these unusually severe strains but came out of the fracas just as straight and undamaged as it had been before the accident.

But there are disadvantages to glass that have not as yet been overcome satisfactorily. As stated, glass is more resilient and powerful, ounce-for-ounce, than bamboo. Strangely enough, this is actually a disadvantage. When it comes to building taper and action into a rod, the lively material makes adding the refinements to a high-grade rod very difficult indeed. Once a glass rod section has been removed from the mold, that section is completed in so far as benchwork is concerned. The action and taper of a bamboo rod section—as it is when it comes from the gluing room—can be shaped and altered by an experienced rodmaker until casting perfection is attained. Not so with glass. This material permits no benchwork. You use it as it happens to be and that is that.

For some reason, the action of the glass fly rods that are being put out nowadays tends to be pretty much confined to the top two-thirds of the rod. In other words, most of them are definitely top-action rods. Of course, this is merely a matter of opinion, but it has always seemed to us that top-action rods are an abomination. And that statement applies, straight across the board, from 6 feet to 10 feet. The action in such a rod is far too fast for accuracy; and when it comes to lengthening line, the softer top action bogs down with the extra weight and the casting is actually done with the lower two-thirds of the rod. That was the trouble with the Hewitt "steep taper." It is high time that makers of glass rods learned this basic truth. So when you are selecting a fly rod, no matter what length and weight, keep this in mind: avoid top-action rods.

Another disadvantage of glass is the evident difficulty the makers have in providing a rod with a good, soft "hooking tip." Consider, for example, the measurements of four 8-foot trout rods, two of bamboo and two of glass. The bamboo rod tips calibrated .074 inch and .076 inch, while the glass rods measured .096 inch and .098 inch—approximately 20 percent heavier than the bamboo. This thicker rod tip not only provides too rigid a base for sure hooking, but the extra bulk sets up considerably more air resistance at the completion of a cast, requiring more power in the lower rod to push the tip through to the finish. Obviously, this does not make for finer finesse in casting a line and fly lightly.

The makers of glass rods also have the distressing tendency to utilize too much of the latent power in glass when setting up a trout rod. An 8-foot bamboo trout rod normally uses an E line; the equivalent rod in glass requires a heavy D or a C line to put it to work. Here again, this does not facilitate delicate casting of a dry fly. Thus, to avoid too much line disturbance on the water, it is necessary to lengthen the leader, a thing that is not always compatible with small-stream fishing.

Selecting Your Rod

The easy way to test action in a fly rod is to hold the grip of the assembled rod firmly in both hands, the rod pointing directly away from you (Plate 11). Then, keeping the

Plate 11. Testing rod action on the lawn of his Pennsylvania home, John Alden Knight braces elbows on hips while holding rod pointing directly away from him. Holding his hands and arms rigid, he waves the tip back and forth slowly to gain a full-action picture of this 9½-foot Winston semi-parabolic taper.

grip rigidly held, wave the tip of the rod back and forth, parallel to the floor. You can look along the rod as it bends and see the exact taper and action. In any rod, regardless of size, it is well to have the action or bending come right down into the grip itself.

Once you have satisfied yourself as to the action or taper, look at the guides. Make sure that no varnish or lacquer is on the guides. Casting soon wears off this soft covering to a knife edge, which will ruin a good line in short order. Some factories, particularly those which turn out cheaper rods, have the deplorable habit of dipping rod sections to give them the finished protective coat. This means that the guides, as well as the rod section, all get a coat of varnish or lacquer. Keep this in mind. For fresh water, steel guides are satisfactory, but for salt water, stainless steel, phosphor bronze, or anodized guides are mandatory.

Next look at the ferrules. Spun ferrules are inexpensive to manufacture. With bamboo rods, spun ferrules, being of the nonwaterproof variety, are a liability rather than an asset. On glass rods, where waterproofing is no longer important, spun ferrules are all right for awhile. Some companies now are using them with a ring of rubber or a rubberlike composition installed near the end of the male ferrule. This insures snug fit for awhile, but, being soft, the ring will wear out. Then your ferrule will need repair or replacement. This is not a serious matter or is it expensive. The trouble is that the ferrule is apt to let go at critical times, say on a long trip in the north woods. You are much better off to make sure that your rod is equipped with reliable bronze or German silver ferrules, lathe-turned, and fitted to exact tolerance. But here is an item about ferrules for use in salt water—salt water, particularly of the southern variety, is *extremely* corrosive. German silver, excellent in fresh water, corrodes in salt water. Thus, the anodized ferrules are preferable by far.

And while you are looking at ferrules, be sure to take a real close look at the diameters of the rod material directly above and below the ferrules. The basic reason for shouldered ferrules—the reason they were invented—was to enable the rodmaker to use rod sections of the same diameter directly above and directly below the metal of the ferrules. In good bamboo rods, the diameter of the upper section is rarely more than .006 inch smaller than the diameter of the lower section where it joins the ferrule. Top tolerance in bamboo between the upper and lower sections where they join the ferrule is .009 inch.

But glass is so much stronger than bamboo, so much more difficult to break, that the makers of glass rods are sometimes inexcusably careless about their diameters. The result is that some two-piece fly rods in glass are put out by reputable firms with a variance in diameters above and below the ferrules of as much as .036 inch. In glass, that rod probably will last a long time; in bamboo, it wouldn't stand a half hour of dry-fly casting. If there is more than a variance of .010 inch, put that rod back in the rack. To enable you to make your measurements, any good sporting-goods store will surely have either a micrometer or a line and leader gauge handy.

Reel seats nowadays are fairly well standardized. No longer do we have to put up with slip rings which depend upon friction to keep them in place. Today, almost all reel seats are of the locking type which screw down tightly and hold your reel in place until you wish to dismount it.

The grip on a rod is an optional affair. "Shaped grips" are not desirable. Neither are thumb rests or flattened spots on which to place the thumb and fingers. Probably the best all-around grip for any type of rod is the old reliable cigar-shaped grip. This grip, made of cork rings (that's important—beware of laminated sheet-cork grips), accommodates itself to any size hand and lends itself to the unhampered use of the free-wrist grip, to be discussed later.

There is one final check which you should apply to any fly rod that may strike your fancy—and this concerns inequality of power in a section. In the high-grade bamboo rods, the rodmakers usually take care of this imperfection by the judicious use of benchwork. But with a glass rod, once the rod sections leave the mold, no corrections can be made.

When a rod section leaves the mold or the gluing room, it rarely flexes evenly in any direction. In other words, there is almost always a "high side"—a position in which the section seems to have more power than it has in any other position. This inequality of power in a section can be caused by any number of things—careless assembly of bamboo strips or variance in the texture of the bamboo itself; slight overwrap in a glass tubular section or unequal distribution of glass fibers around the mandrel in the mold. Regardless of cause, the fact remains that few, very few, rod sections come to the finishing room perfectly balanced.

Finding the High Side

As stated, with good Tonkin cane to work with, this inequality of power can be corrected with benchwork. But with a glass rod, the section must be used or discarded; it can't be altered. So, unless the section is *too* much out of balance, the rodmaker locates the high side; then he marks the section so that the girls in the winding room will mount the guides *opposite* that high side. Well, that's all

Plate 12. The high side of a fly rod is discovered by rolling the section over the palm of the hand while it is under pressure. As it moves, it will jump as it reaches the high side of the section.

right, providing the inequality is not too pronounced. It gives the rod slightly more casting power than it otherwise would have for its weight. But if the high side is too much out of balance, then the rod is quite apt to cast off-line, much like a five-strip bamboo rod. Then, too, the girls in the winding room, or the rodmaker, may have missed the high side entirely. Should this be the case, the rod definitely will cast off-line. On short casts this is not too critical, but on long casts a rod that casts off-line can be a sore trial indeed.

The way to check on the assembly of a fly rod is this (see Plate 12): place the *heavy end* of a rod section on a flat surface, such as a counter or a table. Lay the *light end* of the section on the palm of your left hand and then tilt the section to an angle of about 45 degrees with the flat surface on which it rests. Now place the fingers of your right hand on the center of the rod section and press down so that the section is bent slightly. Then roll the section, still bent, back and forth under the fingers of your right hand. Should there be a high side in the section, as you roll it you will find a distinct tendency for the section to "jump" under your fingers. In this way you can locate the high side exactly. Then check to see that the guides are mounted on the opposite side. If the jump is too pronounced, too severe, the best thing is to forget about that rod and look at another one.

That just about covers the generalities when you are looking at new rods. Now let's consider certain types of rods for certain types of fishing.

Trout Rods

For small-stream fishing, the longest rod compatible with the casting job in hand is always the rod to use. Some anglers insist that a 7-foot rod or even a 6-foot rod is ideal for small streams. But despite their insistence, it is not the length of the cast that controls your choice; instead, it is the ease with which line and fly can be controlled once the cast has been made. It is perfectly possible to cast 60 or 70 feet with a 6-foot rod. Actually, it is possible to cast 50 feet or more with no rod at all, simply holding the line in your hand. But once the cast has been made, what about pick-up or striking a rising fish? The longer rod makes pick-up and striking infinitely easier than the shorter rod. Thus, for small streams, a rod of 7 feet 9 inches or 8 feet makes a more usable tool than the shorter rod.

For larger streams, the trout rivers, the logical rod should certainly not be less than 8 feet 6 inches long. One of these, in the semiparabolic action, will give you all the distance you need and there is enough length to facilitate both pick-up and striking. In addition, a rod of 8 feet 6 inches will handle short casts every bit as well as one of 8 feet or 7 feet 6 inches. There is no need to handicap yourself by using a shorter rod than is absolutely necessary.

Bass-Bug Rods

Bass-bug fishing has been responsible for more confusion and fallacies in fly-rod design than any other single factor since the days of Izaak Walton. This type of fishing, to be done effectively, should be at distances of 60 feet or more. Usually, bass-bug casting is done along a shore line, and this means that accuracy is all-important. Also, bass-bug fishing is, as a general rule, an all-day job, where the caster keeps on banging that bug into pockets, coves, etc., hour after hour. Obviously, either the caster must have the hand of a blacksmith or he must have a rod that is not too punishing on the casting hand.

Many manufacturers seem to ignore these basic facts. They keep on putting out what they call "bass-action" rods—9 feet long, stiff, clubby things, usually decidedly of the top-action variety. No matter *who* the caster may be or how strong his casting hand, an hour's workout with one of these ungainly bass-action rods will reduce that casting hand to the texture of wet spaghetti.

The manufacturers of bass-action rods make the common error of confusing stiffness or rigidity with power. However, a stiff rod with most of the usable action in the upper one third does not begin to transmit the power to the casting line that is delivered by a rod of equal weight with an action that comes clear down into the hand grip. Remember this when you are selecting a bass-bug rod, and steer clear of those "bass-action" atrocities.

Bass-bug fishing, to be done properly, requires the absolute tops in tackle. Don't make the mistake of confusing bass-bug tackle with inexpensive equipment. As a rule, a good bass-bug rod will cost more than a good trout rod. To do accurate casting hour after hour at distances of 60 feet or more requires good equipment. Two of the best bass-bug rods to come to our attention are, respectively, 9 feet 9 inches and 10 feet long. They are slow rods, with the action well distributed throughout the entire length. Both handle heavy forward-taper lines. They will pick up 50 feet of line with ease. Once the line is extended in the back cast, all that is needed on the part of the caster is to give the big rod a shove and then let it do the work for him.

Admittedly, slow rods of 9 feet 9 inches or 10 feet place a rather high premium on correct timing, a gift that the average caster does not have. The best thing is to compromise and settle on a rod of 9 feet 6 inches in length, *reasonably* slow, with the action well distributed through the entire rod. In the bass-bug rod, the semiparabolic taper is not desirable, since it places too much of a load on the casting hand. If you get one with uniform or "circular" taper, your days on bass waters will be happy ones.

Salmon Rods

In common with bass-bug rods, salmon rods should be long and reasonably slow, with the action well distributed throughout the entire rod. After all, since most salmon fishing is of the wet-fly variety, there is little need for much false casting. If you plan to do some dry-fly fishing for salmon, you had best carry an extra rod, somewhat shorter and slightly faster. It is well to have both rods equipped with the auxiliary butt that can be carried in your pocket while casting and then slipped into place when needed. The late Edward R. Hewitt used fly rods that were 10 feet long—big, slow rods that had plenty of power. For dry fly he dropped back to 9 feet 6 inches, which is slightly faster. The late Richard Carley Hunt, a famous salmon fisherman, carried with him a battery of six Leonard rods, all of them 10 feet 6 inches in length. These, too, were slow, powerful rods for use on big salmon rivers. For dry fly, he used a 10-foot Leonard, slightly faster but not much.

These rods, of course, were of bamboo. Today (and let's face it) is the day of glass. Few companies turn out glass fly rods more than 9 feet long. They feel, evidently, that 9 feet will do everything for a caster that he may need, no matter what style of fishing he is doing. The fact remains, however, that what 9 feet will do, 9½ feet will do better, more accurately, and with far less effort. So for salmon, with glass fly rods, 9½ feet is preferable for wet fly, dropping back to 9 feet for dry fly. The extension butt is optional.

Salt-Water Rods

Fly rods were not in general use in salt water until 1947 when it was learned that bonefish would take a well-placed streamer fly. At that time there were few guides in South Florida who had so much as seen a fly rod, much less used one. But they learned quickly, and it was not long before the demand for bonefish rods kept factories busy. Gradually the quality of salt-water fly-rod tackle improved. Today you can find excellent fly-rod gear for salt water in the good tackleshops.

At first, fresh-water tackle was used in salt-water fishing. That was all there was to use; salt-water fly rods were not made in 1947, except in rare cases of special orders. But fresh-water rods—bass-bug rods and salmon rods—were simply not up to the job in hand. Rather quickly, the rod companies began turning out salt-water fly rods, both in bamboo and glass. The first of these were not particularly good rods, but the quality soon improved as manufacturers learned what was needed.

Actually, the main deterrent in the development of fly-rod gear for salt water was the difficulty in finding reels that would stand up under the heavy strains imposed on them by those tough game fish of lower Florida and the Bahamas. Today, reels are better, far better, than they were in 1947, but they still leave much to be desired. A tough, smooth, nonoscillating drag on a salt-water reel is a thing of beauty and a joy forever—if you can find one. To be sure, reels are improving, but they still have the distressing habit of letting you down at crucial times.

Today, salt-water fly rods are divided into two classifications—the bonefish rod and the heavy-duty or "flat" rod used for tarpon, jack crevalle, big snook, etc.

The bonefish rod in bamboo should be 9½ feet, the action slightly faster than the bass-bug rod but well distributed throughout the entire rod. In this rod, the semiparabolic action is good. Casting for bonefish is done only when the fish is sighted and the guide places the skiff into proper casting position. The slow, semiparabolic action provides both accuracy and extra distance—two vital requisites for this type of fishing.

In glass, you probably can get by with 9 feet, but 9½ feet is better by far, providing you can find it. Again, let us caution you against the top-action rods that many companies are turning out. Semiparabolic action *demands* that the action or bending comes clear down into the hand grip; that is one of its inherent characteristics. You can't be too careful in selecting a bonefish rod. It must be accurate and reasonably powerful. A fast, top-action rod simply will not do the job for you. Casting to a feeding bonefish is nearly always a one-cast operation; rarely do you get a second crack at him. If the fly or line alights too close, the fish will flush; if the cast is wide so that the fish does not see it, as often as not the pick-up for a second cast will alarm him and that is that.

Of course, your bonefish rod is not limited to use on bonefish. It is also ideal for fishing for feeding redfish which are cruising the shallow sand flats. It is also good for "blind casting" the channels and potholes for sea trout. This casting is not continuous, but sporadic. You cast out one pothole or channel and then rest your hand while you move on to the next one. Also, the bonefish rod is useful for casting a mangrove shore line for snook. Using a heavy-duty rod for this type of fishing—repeated casting—would put your casting hand out of commission in short order.

In the heavy-duty or "flat" rods (so named for the sand flats on which they are used), you need bulk and power. These rods are seldom used for "blind casting." Almost always you are casting to fish that you can see. But these fish are apt to be anything from a 12- or 15-pound jack crevalle (than which there is no rougher citizen in salt water) or a king-size snook that you *must* keep out of the mangrove roots, to a tarpon weighing better than 100 pounds. Most tournament regulations allow you a 12-pound leader point in salt water. For heavy-duty fishing, you want a rod that will enable you to apply full pressure at all times. If you are not fishing in a tournament, you probably will be using a 20-pound point or better on your leader. You need a rod that will enable you to take full advantage of this comparatively heavy terminal tackle. Remember, when you are playing a heavy fish, a good share of the time your hands will be (or should be) in the "lock" position—one hand halfway up the butt joint of the rod and the other braced firmly against the lower part of the reel seat. To be done effectively, this requires a bulky rod with a substantial butt joint.

In addition to the fish we have named above, many of the more adventurous salt-water fly-rod handlers have found that there are other species that can be whipped on heavy-duty fly tackle, the blessings of good fortune being on the angler's side. There is a wealth of fun to be found on the offshore reefs on both the Atlantic and Pacific coasts for such fish as dolphin, albacore, bonito, king mackerel, sharks, even the smaller billfish. You need never fear that heavy-duty fly tackle is not up to *any* task to which you may put it—it is truly a deadly light tackle weapon.

Best stick to glass for this type of fishing. Nine feet or, even better, 9 feet 6 inches in uniform taper—not top action —will do the job for you.

FUNDAMENTALS OF FLY CASTING

WHILE fly casting is nowadays divided into the following distinct classifications—trout, wet fly and dry fly; salmon, wet fly and dry fly; bass bug; bonefish and "sand-flat casting"; heavy-duty casting; tournament, accuracy and distance—the fundamentals of fly casting are applicable to each classification. Master the basic rules, and your chances to become a good caster are excellent, always providing that you are willing to practice. Ignore the fundamentals, and the probabilities are that never, so long as you live, will you become a good caster.

The first thing to learn in fly casting—and it does not matter whether you are a beginner or an angler with years of experience—is how to hold a fly rod correctly. If you are a golfer, you know the importance of the correct grip. The same holds true in tennis; to handle a racket effectively you must know how to hold it correctly. The same basic fact applies to fly casting.

Fifty or more years ago, fly casters were taught to cast with forearm and wrist alone, the upper arm—elbow to shoulder—held rigidly against the side. To insure this posi-

53

tion, beginners were made to practice with a book or a handkerchief held in the armpit of the casting arm. The rod was held in the fingers (not against the palm) and the thumb was placed firmly on top of the rod (the spot opposite the side on which the reel is attached).

As you read the preceding paragraph again, pick up any convenient object—a pencil or a fountain pen will do— and let it serve as a rod grip. Hold it in the manner described, thumb on top, and the grip held in the fingers. Keep the upper arm held rigidly against your side. Now, execute the motions of fly casting. Considering the entire possible arc of rod movement as the upper half of a clock face, begin the back cast at ten o'clock (that's what the old instructions always told you to do) and finish the back cast at the one-o'clock position. You will note that most of the rod movement is effected by movement of the forearm. After the rod has moved through an arc of 15 or 20 degrees, you will find that the thumb-on-top grip locks the wrist so that it can go no farther. When you attempt to inject any wrist movement into the cast—to aid the impulse given by the forearm—the tendency is to have the back cast stop at the three o'clock position instead of at the one o'clock position. In short, you have cramped and handicapped your casting arm to the point where free, unhampered movement is almost impossible.

Having watched many hundreds of casters in action on stream and lake, it became an actual challenge to find out why 99 out of a hundred of them were such abominably bad casters. What fault did they have in common that made it impossible for them to cast even passably well? The answer came eventually. The fault lay in the grip and the back cast.

It is an axiom in fly casting that if you throw a back cast

correctly, it is almost impossible to throw a bad forward cast. Conversely, if the back cast is *not* thrown as it should be, then it is exceedingly difficult to throw a good forward cast. But in order to throw a good back cast you must hold your rod correctly.

The Free-Wrist Grip

A fly rod is actually supported by the thumb and index finger of the casting hand. Additional support is provided by the other three fingers which hold the grip against the palm and the heel of the hand. Plate 13 shows the correct way to hold a fly rod. You will note that the thumb is at the side of the grip, not on top. This places the lower joint of the index finger on top of the grip. Actually there are four pressure points—the side of the thumb, the side of the

Plate 13. The free-wrist grip is the modern way to hold a fly rod. Allowing his thumb and forefinger to form a V on top of the rod grip, the caster brings the full, free leverage of the wrist into play on cast.

Plate 14. This clock face shows the follow-through necessary to hold a back cast up high where it counts. Note that the caster turns to check his back cast, an excellent practice while learning control.

index finger, the lower joint of the index finger (where it joins the palm proper) and the heel of the palm. The other three fingers of the casting hand serve merely to hold the grip in place.

Now—once you have the grip comfortably in mind— consider your casting arm. Instead of holding the upper arm rigidly against the side, allow it to relax and hold the rod slightly to the side instead of directly in front of you. This position enables you to put the free-wrist grip into full play.

The High Back Cast

Assume that the line is extended on the water in front of you. First, extend your casting hand and forearm slightly in front of you *at the nine o'clock position,* not ten o'clock. Now, start the rod tip up through the allowable arc of movement, gradually accelerating its speed as it moves. As you near the one o'clock position, the free-wrist grip will enable you to flip the rod tip so that the line will be thrown into the air behind you *well above the horizontal.*

The line should start its rearward journey *at least 30 degrees above the horizontal* (see Plate 14).

The reason for this should be obvious. The force of gravity is always working. As the line travels to the rear, gravity pulls it down. By the time it is fully extended, you will have lost a goodly share of that 30-degree angle you had at the start. Actually, by the time you start the forward cast, your line is only slightly above the horizontal. And this is where it should be. If it falls too far below the horizontal, then you will have trouble getting that forward cast up, over and out, the way it should go.

And what about your casting arm? Old-school instructions to the contrary, it makes little difference what you do with your casting arm as long as it is comfortable and its position allows full play for the free-wrist grip. You can keep it low if that is where you want it for comfort, but you will find that by lifting it slightly you will have better control of the line. Eventually—and this is particularly true of long casts—you will find your casting arm extended back and up at an angle of about 45 degrees. In this way, the arm actually acts as a continuation or extension of the rod. Unorthodox? Not at all; merely sensible.

When you are practicing the high back cast (Plate 15), it is best to start with a fairly short line, say 25 feet or so, exclusive of the leader. Pick the line up in the manner described and toss it into the high back cast. As the line travels to the rear, turn your head and watch its progress. *This is important.* By doing so, not only do you learn to put that back cast up there where it belongs; you also learn timing—how long it takes that line to extend itself to the rear. Without learning these two things, you will never become a finished caster. So don't try to handle too much line at the beginning. Practice with a fairly short line at

Plate 15. Throwing a high back cast, the junior author aims a full 30 degrees above the horizontal. Turning with the cast is a good way to check proper line and hand position. Note full casting arm extension at the very completion of the cast.

Plate 16. The elbow "floats" at the start of forward cast delivery, dropping down and through the cast as the hand, rod and arm generate power.

Plate 17. A well-executed forward cast is the result of a good back cast. Aimed at a point some 3 feet above the water, a good forward cast becomes an acceleration, allowing the line, fly and leader to "turn over" on their way to the target.

first until you master the fundamentals. Distance casting will come in good time.

The Forward Cast

The forward cast is relatively simple, always providing that the back cast has been thrown properly, up there where it should be. As you watch the back cast travel toward its completion, the rod tip should follow through with the cast until it comes almost to two o'clock, so that the arc of movement is lengthened. Just before the line extends itself completely to the rear (Plate 16), start the forward motion of the rod tip. Like the back cast, the forward cast is a gradually accelerated motion, ending with a definite flip of the upper rod (Plate 17). Aim the cast at a point about 3 feet above the level of the water, this to give the line, leader and fly time to "turn over" at the completion of the cast while the balance of the line falls. As stated, gravity is always working against you; you must make allowances for it. And again, always remember

that if a good back cast is made, then it is exceedingly difficult to throw a bad forward cast.

Timing

Timing can be described most easily as "the rhythm of
fly casting." When you throw the high back cast, you have
learned that there is a pause in the motion of the rod
while the line travels to the rear. This pause is actually the
key to timing. If the pause is of too short duration, part of
the line will start its forward journey while the balance still
travels toward the rear. One motion tends to neutralize
the other, and this causes loss of power in the cast. If your
timing has been too faulty, the cast will not complete itself.
Again, if you wait too long, the line will drop below the
horizontal and you will have trouble getting the forward
cast up, over and out. More often than not this results in a
bad forward cast. In addition, too long a wait causes the
line to fall toward the water, thereby losing tension against
the rod with a resultant loss of power. One of the absolute
essentials of good casting is good timing. That is the reason it is wise to turn your head and watch the line as you
practice the high back cast. Later on, as you progress into
the advanced stages of fly casting, you will now and then
have trouble making the line do what you want it to.
Almost always this is a matter of faulty timing. When this
happens, it is a simple matter to turn your head, watch your
back cast, and thus correct your timing on the spot.

Some casters, still in the beginner class, find it useful to
count, in order to check timing—one—two—three. The best
way to do this is to stretch out the word "one" through the
entire movement of the rod during the back cast. "Two"
comes at the completion of the back cast as the rod starts
forward. And "three" comes at the completion of the for-

ward cast. As you learn to lengthen line so that the spacing of your timing becomes more pronounced, it is sometimes helpful to insert the word "and" between counts—one-and-two-and-three. You will soon learn, however, that counting is not necessary. With enough practice, you will reach the point where you can place your fly lightly, and as it should be placed, at a given spot and in the desired manner without giving thought to the separate parts of the casting motion. Then, and not until then, have you become a fly caster.

4

A WET fly, as you know, simulates or suggests a drowned insect, one that has come to grief in the riffles and has been washed beneath the surface. Or it may simulate the behavior of a newly hatched fly making its way from the stream bottom toward the surface. In either case, when fishing a wet fly, it is necessary for the caster to have complete control of his line at all times. In one instance, the fly must be allowed to "drift dead," as a drowned insect would naturally drift. In the other, the fly must be well submerged first, then brought toward the surface in erratic, well-spaced movements. In either case, the line must always be under full control. A dragging wet fly which swishes across a riffle pocket, swept by the current, as a rule accomplishes little in the matter of catching fish. By the same token, a submerged fly which drags steadily and unnaturally across-current is rarely effective. To fish a wet fly well, the angler must know how to cast and handle his line.

Casting a Straight Line

While at first glance wet-fly casting seems to be a rather simple and easy process, this is not entirely true. A great deal of your success in wet-fly fishing depends upon your ability to cast a straight line. This may sound like a strange statement, but it isn't. Most casters regard the "trick casts"—such as the positive and negative curves, the roll cast, Galway cast, etc.—as being difficult to learn. Compared to the straight line, they are relatively simple. Casting the straight line is the most difficult of all fly-rod casts.

The reason for this is fairly obvious if you will consider what a fly rod does as it goes through the motion of throwing the forward cast. To illustrate, suppose you are handling 50 or 60 feet of line, enough to provide the needed line load to put *all* of your rod to work. At the conclusion of the back cast, the forward motion of the rod is started, accelerating gradually to the final "throwing in" or flip of the upper rod to apply that extra bit of power at the point of release. Exactly what happens at that critical point—the point of release? (See Plates 18 and 19.)

In the average fly rod, there is not enough strength in the upper 10 or 12 inches to deliver all of the power of the cast. When the line is released and starts its forward journey, this upper 10 or 12 inches of rod simply rides along with the line, the actual power of the cast having been delivered from a point somewhat *below* the tip. When the line is free and moving forward on its own, this unused portion of the rod follows through, passes the position where the rod once more is straight, and dips downward slightly but enough to transmit a downward wave or "hump" in the line, so that instead of casting a straight line you are throwing one that is wavy and uneven.

In order to throw a straight line, it is necessary to control or moderate the final flip of the tip section of the rod. This is a rather fine adjustment to which the casting hand must be trained. With too little power applied to the finish of

Plate 18. Extending the back cast on a level plane, the caster puts himself in position to deliver a straight line cast, one of the most important of all wet-fly maneuvers.

Plate 19. A moderation of power on forward cast delivery is necessary to throw a good straight line cast. Here, the junior author delivers 60 feet of line and leader to the target. Note the flat plane of the line belly as well as the tight bow of the cast.

the cast, the cast itself is apt to bog down and fail to complete itself. With too much power applied at the finish, the inevitable follow-through will result with a wavy, crooked line going forward. To strike the happy medium is one of the refinements of good casting. The adjustment varies with the length of line being thrown, and it is not the same with any two fly rods. It can be learned only through practice and experience. It all depends on how willing you are to train your casting hand. Admittedly, this is an unsatisfactory way to describe the procedure of throwing a straight line, but there seems to be no other way to master the knack of doing it, save through trial and error.

Free-Wrist Action on Pick-Up

When discussing fundamentals, the pick-up was described as starting the rod tip back with a gradually accelerated motion. Actually this is only part of the story. No mention was made of wrist action, save to bring out the proper position of the hand for the free-wrist grip. There is another function of this grip that is extremely important, particularly when you are handling a long line.

When starting the pick-up (see Plate 20), it is important that the line get underway as early as possible. Lifting the rod tip does this for you all right when you are handling a short line. At the same time, however, lifting the rod tip uses up a goodly portion of the allowable arc of motion. An easy way to start the line in its rearward motion and to overcome most of the skin friction which the water exerts against a submerged or partially submerged line is as follows. First extend the casting hand out at arm's length in front of you, the rod held parallel to the surface of the water. Strip in line through the guides until there is ten-

Plate 20. A slight lag forward allows the caster's wrist to overcome water skin friction and put his line in motion on beginning of the back cast.

sion on the line. Now, bring the casting hand directly back, almost to a position near the shoulder. At the same time, bend the wrist *slightly forward* as the hand moves back, so that the rod remains parallel to the water. This serves to put the line in motion. Not until the casting hand is drawn back almost to the shoulder is the rod tip started upward (see Plate 21), gradually accelerating until the final flip is made at the one o'clock position, the casting arm going along with the cast and extending up, out and back to give height to the back cast (see Plate 22). This is not a difficult maneuver to learn, but always remember that it must be

Plate 21. The wrist reaches full cock at the beginning of the forward cast delivery. Once again lagging slightly behind the cast, it drives over and through the forward arc to generate full, easy power.

Plate 22. Back cast follow-through lets the rod, hand and arm drift past the rear power generation point of one o'clock to a full extension of the casting arm. This movement increases the allowable arc of motion on the forward cast, letting you handle more line with less effort.

done smoothly, one component part flowing gently and evenly into the next as the cast progresses.

Free-Wrist Action on the Forward Cast

As the back cast completes itself (see Plate 18), the same free-wrist maneuver can be repeated on the forward cast. Instead of starting the rod tip forward to make the line change its direction of flow, start the casting hand and arm forward, tilting the hand *slightly back* as you do so. Not until the hand has once more reached a point opposite the shoulder do you start the rod tip forward. Then the cast is completed with the conventional accelerated motion and the final "throwing in" of the upper rod.

You will find that by employing the free-wrist action on back cast and forward cast you can handle a longer line far more easily than you can with the conventional motions. Also—and this is important—you will find that this method of casting is practically impossible when using the thumb-on-top-of-the-rod grip.

The Follow-Through

Just as the free-wrist action on the pick-up and the start of the forward cast will help you to handle more line than you can use comfortably with the more orthodox method, so will the follow-through on the back cast enable you to handle a longer line by increasing the allowable arc of motion of the fly rod in its forward journey, thereby providing the opportunity to apply more power to the cast. Generally speaking, it is not a good idea to use a long line while fishing the wet fly. However, there are times when the spots you wish to fish cannot be reached with a short line. Then you must know how to handle a long line and handle it well, always under direct control. The follow-through on the back cast will help you to do exactly that.

What is meant by the follow-through on the back cast is this—the pick-up is made as usual, with the final impulse imparted to the line at approximately one o'clock. As explained earlier, to get "full lift" to the back cast, raise the casting arm to a fully extended position about 45 degrees to the rear. As the line travels back, allow the rod tip to drift back with it to the two o'clock or two-thirty position, gradually lowering the elbow of the casting arm as you do so. The reason for lowering the elbow is to make the line drop slightly as it travels to the rear. Remember, the force of gravity always works against you. By lowering the elbow, the rod tip is kept in direct line with the back cast. Thus, when the forward cast is started, direct, full power can be appplied to the forward cast.

A few words of caution—when you are executing the follow-through, care must be taken to apply full power to the back cast at one o'clock, the point of release, *before* the rod tip is permitted to drift back into the follow-through. If you fail to do this and allow the delivery of power and the follow-through to blend into one motion, then, inescapably, a low back cast and consequent trouble will result.

The Backhand Cast

Many times, particularly when you are fishing small streams, obstructions of one sort or another render it difficult to use the forehand cast. Often a strong wind, blowing from right to left, makes forehanded casting not only difficult but dangerous. When such an occasion arises, many anglers have schooled themselves to meet the emergency by learning to cast with the left hand. This expedient may be all right for those who like it. However, a well-trained

Plate 23.   Casting backhand puts the casting forearm almost parallel with the water with the palm of the casting hand aimed directly at the target. As your proficiency increases, this school position can be altered to a lower, and more comfortable, level.

Plate 24.   In action, the backhand cast is as easy to throw as any. Simply adjust your timing to compensate for your position and let your rod and casting hand do the rest.

casting hand can handle a fly rod in any position from parallel to the water on the left side, right through the full 180 degrees.

To learn the backhand cast, raise your casting arm so that the forearm is parallel with the water surface, the back of the hand directly in front of the chin, and the palm facing the direction of the forward cast (see Plate 23). Now, place the rod grip in your casting hand while it is in this position, being careful to use the free-wrist grip, just as you would in forehanded casting.

Execute the pick-up just as you would in forehanded casting, making sure that the back cast is thrown well above the horizontal and delivering all the power you need at the point of release, one o'clock. Following through slightly as the line travels back, wait until the line has extended itself, and then, without altering your position, make the forward cast just as you would with the forehanded cast (see Plate 24).

At first, the backhand cast may seem a bit awkward, but a little practice will show you that it is an easy motion to learn. As you grow used to having the rod on the left side, you can alter the original extreme hand and arm position used in learning the cast. Lower the arm to a more comfortable position as your proficiency in the cast increases. Some anglers execute the backhand cast very well with the casting hand held at waist level. But remember this always—no matter where you hold your rod, right or left side, *invariably the palm of the hand should face the direction of the cast.*

The Horizontal Cast

This cast is useful only once in awhile when you wish to place your fly or lure under overhanging obstructions or

Plate 25. Thrown slightly high, the horizontal back cast fights gravity while it holds a long line free of the water. The elbow of the casting arm follows the cast slightly to the rear and cocks for forward delivery.

Plate 26. A horizontal forward cast, shown here at the moment of full forward power, is aimed slightly higher than the horizontal. This holds the line in the air longer to allow for full cast turn-over.

when an overhead back cast is not practical. To be sure, there are several special casts that can be used to solve such difficulties. These will be discussed later on. But the horizontal cast is often useful, particularly when you are using a short line.

In the horizontal cast, either forehand or backhand, the rod is held almost parallel to the surface of the water. The line is picked up in the usual manner and the back cast is thrown *slightly above the horizontal* to allow for the pull of our old enemy, gravity (see Plate 25). The final impulse is given the line, as always, at one o'clock (see Plate 26). It is best not to follow through too far with this cast. Simply handle it in orthodox manner, without elaboration.

All of the foregoing casts are necessary in wet-fly fishing. With all of them you can throw that always-desirable straight line which gives you control of your flies at all times. Learn them well, and your days on the streams with the wet fly will be pleasant and productive ones. Fail to learn them, so that your casts are faulty and unsure, and as much as 50 percent of good fishing time may be wasted.

DRY-FLY CASTING $\rangle$ 5

WHEN a wet-fly fisherman first changes over to dry fly, he is confronted with two new casting problems. Because of the fact that the dry fly is usually fished upstream, just as soon as the fly alights on the water it begins to drift back toward the angler. Slack line begins to accumulate, and this must be taken care of immediately so that the angler is always in position to strike a fish that rises to his fly. There should be no delay in the strike; thus, the line always should be under direct control.

When the fly is picked up from the water, droplets of water always adhere to both line and fly, and these must be shaken off, even though the fly has been oiled and the line thoroughly dressed. Thus, the line and the fly must be "false-cast" several times before being recast.

False Casting

False casting consists of remaking the back cast before the forward cast has settled to the water. Done correctly, false casting involves a somewhat different technique than simple wet-fly casting. Too many anglers use the same

Plate 27. False casting consists of remaking the cast before it has fallen into the water. Note that the forward cast shown here has begun before the back cast has completed itself. Used for aim and line lengthening, the false cast is mandatory in dry-fly fishing, as it gives the line and fly time to shake loose droplets of water before final delivery.

motions and timing in false casting that they use in wet-fly casting. The result is that their false casting is slow, labored and inefficient for the purpose for which it is intended—to shake water droplets from the line, leader and fly.

To false-cast properly, the pick-up is made in the usual way and the line sent to the rear, being released at the one o'clock position. Here the similarity to wet-fly casting ceases. In the first place, the back cast is not thrown into the high back cast. Instead, it is thrown straight back. As the line travels back, let the rod tip drift with it into a rather exaggerated follow-through, so that the rod actually passes the two o'clock position. Then, before the line has extended itself, start the forward cast (see Plate 27). Aim the forward cast at a point 4 or 5 feet above the surface of the water; follow through with the rod tip almost to the ten o'clock position, and then—just before the forward cast has completed itself—begin the back cast once more. This process should be repeated several times. The final back cast should be thrown high, just as in wet-fly casting, allowing the cast to extend itself almost completely, at which time the final forward cast is made, aimed at the desired target and about 3 feet above the surface so that leader and fly have time to "turn over" and thus place the fly lightly on the surface.

If the false cast is handled in this way, *with the timing shortened somewhat*, both forward and back, and a little more power put into each motion than is actually needed, the line, leader and fly will travel in what is known as the "figure eight." Speeding up the timing causes the fly to turn over, forward and back, in a fairly wide curve instead of ending its journey with a sharp snap. The added speed which has been built up by use of the follow-through and extra power will throw off the water droplets from your terminal tackle so that line and fly will float when recast to the water.

Dry-fly fishing is really the enemy of sound timing. Fully 75 percent of the casts that you make while dry-fly fishing are false casts. If the angler recognizes this fact and learns to vary his timing to suit the needs of false casting and final accuracy casting, his troubles will be few in number. But if he falls into the habit of allowing a false cast to complete itself into a final accuracy cast, the result is usually sloppy and inaccurate. The wide "bow" of the "figure eight" lacks precision, and the slightest puff of wind will throw it off line. Be sure to separate the two casts in your mind and don't let one encroach upon the other.

The Bow

The easiest way to define the "bow" is the distance between the top and bottom *of the curve* in the line as it travels through the air, either forward or back (see Plate 28). A good caster *must* be able to regulate the span of the bow at will. This ability is an exceedingly useful asset in just about every form of casting. It enables the dry-fly angler to throw forehand and backhand curve casts, both positive and negative. It allows the bass-bug fisherman, the salt-water fisherman and the tournament caster to take full advantage of a favorable wind or to "cheat" an adverse wind. Being able to widen or tighten the span of the bow often spells the difference between success and failure.

To tighten or "flatten" the bow, the easy way is as follows. Toss the line into the high back cast after the pick-up, extending the casting arm up and back for the

Plate 28. A wide bow is usually thrown down or across the wind, *letting the middle rod apply the power* while the cast rides out high and wide.

Plate 29. A tight bow is driven into the target with the tip thrown into full power a bit later than usual, causing the cast to rifle in low and hard.

"high lift" at the point of release (see Plate 29). Allow the rod tip to follow through as the cast travels rearward. Gradually lower the casting elbow as the line travels back, to compensate for the drop caused by gravity and to permit the application of direct power to the forward cast.

Start the forward cast just an instant before the line is fully extended to the rear, using slightly more power than needed. To complete the forward cast, apply the final flip or "throwing in" of the upper rod at a point slightly beyond the usual point of release. Always be careful not to overdo the application of power at the point of release, because the upper line of the bow is apt to foul the lower line while coming through. Just as when throwing the straight line, a little practice and experimentation will train your casting hand so that you can throw a tight bow without difficulty.

The wide bow is executed with an entirely different technique. Instead of throwing the usual high back cast after the pick-up, the back cast is thrown only slightly above the horizontal. Follow through somewhat with the rod tip, but do not raise the casting arm above the normal position. Instead of waiting for the line to extend itself completely to the rear, the timing should be hurried somewhat in starting the forward cast, similar to the timing in false casting.

Now here is the vital point of difference between this and any other cast that you will learn to make. As you start the forward cast, *apply the power of the cast with the middle rod only,* omitting the final flip or throwing in of the upper rod at the completion of the forward motion. If done correctly, this method will produce an extremely wide bow. Of course, the cast can be modified later on to meet the needs of the occasion. Once you have learned the trick of applying power with the middle rod only, the cast can be modified as desired.

The Grasshopper Cast

In dry-fly fishing, it is always desirable to have the fly turn over at the completion of a cast and float lightly to the surface of the water somewhat ahead of the leader and the end of the line. With 30 or 40 feet of line, this is no particular problem. But when you are using 50 or 60 feet of line, it is often difficult to hold that much line off the water while the fly turns over at the end of the cast. It is with the longer casts that the grasshopper cast is especially useful.

In throwing the grasshopper cast, it is a good plan to use not less than 50 feet of line. The back cast should be fairly high and the rod tip should follow through with the cast to about two o'clock. Drop the elbow as the back cast nears completion and then shove a little more power into the forward cast than is actually needed to make the fly reach its destination. At the point of release, the upper rod should be thrown into the final flip a bit more emphatically than would be normal (see Plate 30). This will cause the tip to carry through and create a downward "hump" in the line which moves forward with the cast. When this hump strikes the water, the forward motion of the line is checked, and in this way added speed is imparted to the line on the upper side of the bow. The end of the line, the leader and the fly will then snap up, over and out and the fly will alight gently on the surface of the water slightly ahead of the leader and line. For quiet water, in which trout always are shy and scary, a long line is a necessity and the grasshopper cast is quite useful under these conditions. It is not

Plate 30. Grasshoppering a cast is done by throwing in the tip a bit harder than usual, causing the line to strike the water between the caster and the target. Done correctly, the upper part of the bow will extend out and over, allowing the fly to settle gently ahead of the leader and forward section of the line. This is an extremely handy maneuver when handling a long line with dry fly.

→

Plate 31. A positive curve cast hooks away from the casting palm to the left. Thrown off a tight bow delivery, the curve is imparted to the cast by raising the rod tip to check forward line speed at completion.

a difficult cast to learn and it can be thrown either fore-hand or backhand.

Curve Casts

In dry-fly fishing, it is always preferable to have the fly come to the fish without letting the line and leader drift over it first. To be sure, a great many fish have been caught which have had a good look at both line and leader before seeing the fly. But your chances of "lining down" a fish are all too good if the line drifts over it first. It is for this reason that the curve casts have been developed. There are two distinct types of curve casts—the positive curve and the negative curve. These casts are thrown with entirely different techniques and must therefore be considered separately.

Positive Curve Cast

A positive curve cast is one which curves away from the side of the casting hand. If you are a right-handed caster, the positive curve will swing to the left. A backhand positive curve will swing to the right, since the casting hand is held to the left of the body.

To throw a forehand positive curve, make the rod move through a plane that is about 45 degrees off the perpendicular. Always remembering to use the high back cast, throw a tight bow, with plenty of extra power, and aim the cast at least 3 or 4 feet above and to the right of your target. As the fly reaches the completion of the forward cast, raise the rod tip slightly, to aid in checking forward speed of the line. This motion and the extra power you have applied to the cast will cause the fly to snap around to the left (see Plate 31). The leader will fall to the water in an upstream curve, and the line will alight well to the right of the line of drift of the fly.

This is one cast in which our old enemy, gravity, actually can be made to help so long as you hold the rod at a 45-degree angle. If you make the mistake of holding the rod almost horizontal when you throw a positive curve, you lose gravity's aid and must depend solely upon extra power to snap fly and leader around to the desired position.

The backhand positive curve is thrown exactly the same as the forehand except that the casting hand is held to the left of the body and the fly aimed at a target 3 or 4 feet to the left of the desired spot, since the curve will swing around to the right.

The Negative Curve

It is not always expedient to attempt to throw positive curves. For example, suppose you are using one of the spiders, variants or palmers, and a 9- or a 10-foot leader tapered to 5X. The air resistance of these patterns is so great compared to their weight that it is just about impossible to throw them into a usable positive curve, and a negative curve is needed.

To execute the negative curve, make your rod move through a plane which is only slightly above the horizontal. Don't attempt to toss the high back cast with this cast. Instead, throw the back cast almost in the horizontal plane, following through with the rod tip. In the forward cast, apply power *with the middle rod only,* leaving the upper rod out of the cast just as you do when throwing a wide bow. Apply just enough power to start the line forward, but not enough to complete the cast. The result is a half-hearted attempt with a wide bow which falls to the water

Plate 32. To throw a negative curve cast, keep your back cast low. The forward cast is thrown *with the middle rod only,* resulting in a sloppy, incomplete cast.

Plate 33. No need to go ashore to change from a wet fly to a dry fly. Simply strip the rod and install a spare reel. String up your gear with the butt section tucked inside your waders and then reassemble conveniently on the spot.

before the bow has had a chance to complete itself (see Plate 32). Actually, the cast is an incomplete forward cast.

Of course, you aim this cast at a spot well to the left of your target. And if you find that you have applied too much power to the cast so that the bow may possibly complete itself and "turn over," the cast can be "killed" by following through with the rod tip and at the same time feeding slack line out through the guides.

The negative curve cast usually throws a much more pronounced curve than a positive curve. It is extremely useful for dropping a fly into a pocket on the far side of a fast water run. A fly which is cast into such a pocket with an ordinary cast is almost at once whisked out by the pull of the current. But the large upstream curve of line and leader allows the fly to remain in the pocket long enough to be taken by a trout.

It will pay you to practice the curve casts. Don't wait until you are on the stream to do your practicing. This only wastes good fishing time. You will find that the ability to handle the curves, positive and negative, forehand and backhand, will increase your chances tremendously when it comes to taking fish from spots that are difficult to fish properly. Not too many anglers will take the trouble to learn the curve casts. Thus there are many good trout in the "tough spots" that stay there, week after week, simply because those spots are not fished properly. Learning to handle the curves well gives you a big advantage.

LINE HANDLING

6

IN the foregoing chapters you have probably noted that little mention has been made of line handling. In other words, what does your left hand do with the slack line while your right hand is busy handling the rod? It might now be well to take a close look at the handling of slack line, since it constitutes an important part of fly casting.

When handling a short line—say 25 feet or so—there is little or no problem with slack line. A short line can be picked up and recast with no trouble. But the line should be held by the fingers of the casting hand, since it is not a good plan to cast against the reel. With the free-wrist grip, the rod is supported by the thumb and the index finger. Thus the easy way is to hold the line between the middle finger and the rod grip. In this way the line can be steadied rather gently and is easily released in the event of a strike.

But when you extend your cast to 40 feet or more, slack line will accumulate. This is stripped in through the guides and across the middle finger of the casting hand. With casts of less than 50 feet, not enough slack will accumulate to complicate matters. When you wish to pick up the line for a recast, simply strip in some slack over the middle finger until you have a tight line on what remains in the water. Then, holding the slack with your left thumb and index finger, make your cast as usual and release the slack line *after* the power has been delivered to the forward cast, *not before*.

The Shoot

When you are fishing either dry fly or wet fly, it is often necessary to extend your cast to 60 or 70 feet. With a trout rod, or any rod for that matter, it is unlikely that you will wish to attempt to pick up 60 or 70 feet of line from the water. This means that you will accumulate 25 or 30 feet of slack which has been stripped in through the guides and over the middle finger of the casting hand. What to do with all of this slack line?

There are three schools of thought concerning the handling of slack line. Some men, with a rolling motion of the left hand, bulk the line into a tight ball. Others gather loops of line which are held in the hand. Still others simply allow the slack to fall to the water beside them. The method of building a ball of slack is not good. It is rough on the finish of an expensive line and it encourages tangles which complicate recasting. The loop method is all right, always provided that one loop does not overlap the next. This, too, can result in tangles. The easiest way (although admittedly the sloppiest) is to allow the line to fall into the water beside you.

Let us say you have shortened line so that you can pick up a convenient amount, a length that can be handled without too much effort. As the line travels to the rear in the back cast, allow a limited amount of slack to slide out through the guides and into the back cast. Then on the forward cast, apply enough power to reach the 60- or 70-foot mark, and release the slack *after* you have delivered the power to the cast, *not before*. The slack line will slide out or "shoot" through the guides as the cast travels to its destination (see Plate 34). Allowing the line to shoot through the guides both on the forward cast and the back cast, is known as the "double shoot." It is a handy trick to have up your sleeve when you are throwing a long line, and it simplifies the forward shoot by reducing the amount of slack to be handled. Of course, you must put extra power into the back cast if you plan to use the double shoot. Otherwise the feeding of slack line will "kill" the back cast and allow loose line to accumulate beyond the rod tip, making the forward cast difficult if not impossible.

Handling slack line, while always a problem, soon becomes a matter of course, something you do automatically.

Plate 34. Forming a guide with his thumb and forefinger, the senior author controls slack line handily during the "shoot" of a cast.

Sometimes you will do it one way, sometimes another. For example, when you are fishing dry fly in a small stream, you are casting directly ahead of you, against the current. Under these conditions it is impractical to drop the slack line in the water beside you, since it has the distressing habit of washing down around your legs and becoming entangled with your wading shoes. Then you must revert to the accumulation of loops in your left hand, or worse still, balling-up the slack in your left fist. It is a matter which you must work out for yourself as time goes on, but the solutions to slack-line problems usually come easily.

The Haul

When the back cast is made, the line naturally travels to the rear. As it does so it builds up considerable velocity, particularly when you are using a long line, and this velocity must be checked. The next job is to start the line forward, building up new velocity in the opposite direction. Several means have been developed to accomplish this necessary result—the follow-through, the free-wrist action and of course the high back cast. But with a long line it is often difficult to build up sufficient acceleration and velocity in the forward cast to shove the cast out to its completion, particularly when there is an adverse breeze. Extra initial acceleration is needed, and to get this "the haul" has been developed.

In the haul, the pick-up is made in the usual manner and the line thrown to the rear in the high back cast. You may or may not have used the free-wrist action in the pick-up, but do so if you are handling a long line. Follow through with the rod tip, casting arm fully extended about 45 degrees to the rear. Now, as the line travels rearward and your left thumb and forefinger hold the slack, move your left hand back and up as far as you can reach, even to the stripping guide if your arm is long enough. It makes matters easier if your weight is shifted back to your right foot and the body actually turned so that your chest and shoulders face the rear. Hold this position while the line travels back.

Just before the line completes its rearward journey, start the forward cast—first with the free-wrist action and then with the rod tip. As the rod proper is brought into the cast, yank the left hand down smartly so that its movement ends to the rear of your left knee (see Plate 35). At the same time the rod is brought through, applying full power to the cast. At the point of release, *immediately* after the line has started forward on its own, feed the slack between your left hand and the stripping guide out through the guides in the beginning of the shoot, releasing the slack as you do so. With the use of the haul, you will be surprised at the ease with which you can add extra distance to the forward cast. Admittedly, you don't learn to use the haul in five minutes. To do so takes time and practice. But it is a useful trick to have in your bag, one that is well worth learning.

In ordinary fishing, you can use modified versions of the haul. Once you learn it you will find yourself speeding up the forward cast by using a short haul of 3 or 4 feet. Even with this reduced version, the ease of the forward cast (as compared to identical casts without using the haul) is surprising.

The Double Haul

For handling an extra-long line, the use of the haul can be employed in the pick-up and back cast. Assume that your line is extended out on the water before you. You have stripped in slack until you feel that you can pick

Plate 35. Hauling hard, the junior author drives a long cast crosswind. The left hand has slashed down and past the left hip, speeding up the forward line momentum to a sharp peak before full release of the cast.

up the remainder and throw it into the high back cast. Now reach out and seize the line just behind the stripping guide. As you make the pick-up, yank down smartly with your left hand, the two motions (right and left hand) blending into one. Next, of course, you move into the motions of the repeated haul to aid your forward cast.

Again, in ordinary fishing with average length of line, you will find yourself using modified versions of the double haul. Once these motions are learned so that they become second nature, you use them to facilitate casting without knowing it.

Corrections As the Cast Progresses

Nobody, and it makes no difference how good a caster he or she may be, makes perfect casts every time. When you stop to consider that a full day of dry-fly fishing may involve as much as 5,000 casts (false casts build up numbers rapidly), it stands to reason that every cast will not be a perfect one. It is possible, however, to salvage a bad cast, and with timely line handling, turn it into a reasonably good cast.

Consider, for example, that you are casting to a target 50 feet or so away from you. This means that you will probably be handling a certain amount of slack line. Instead of allowing this slack to shoot through the guides without any control, it is always a good idea to allow that slack to ride out through a ring formed by the thumb and index finger of your left hand. In effect, this makes an extra guide and gives you instant control of the line at all times. If you find you are going to overcast, you can check the shoot instantly, since you have the line right there in your fingers. If you see that you have not applied enough power to the forward cast or the back cast, you can always correct this by checking the line and shortening the cast so that it will turn over on completion instead of coming down in a "bird's nest."

No two anglers handle line in exactly the same way. Basically, the manner of one is similar to that of the others, but each man develops small modifications to suit his own particular style. We can give you only the fundamentals here. From there on it is up to you.

SPECIAL CASTS

THE fly rod is indeed a tool of multiple use. After you become well acquainted with one, you will find that you will be able to do surprising things with it. When dry-fly fishing, after a little experience, you will be able to place your fly gently and accurately in spots a foot square at distances of from 30 to 50 feet and continue to do so time after time. You are bound to have some bad casts—everybody does. But after you become used to your rod and your line and the balance between the two, you will develop unfailing accuracy that is a knack which stays with you and is not forgotten.

So far, only orthodox casts have been discussed. There are others things that do not conform to the orthodox that can be done with a well-balanced rod and line combination. A fly-rod man should know these casts; they will serve him well in his days on lake, stream or salt-water sand flat. While they may seem difficult at first, they actually are not. Once you have been well-grounded in the fundamentals, the rest comes easy. Remember, the straight line is the toughest cast of all. If you can throw that one consistently, you should have no difficulty with the others.

The Roll Cast

The roll cast has mainly been designed for wet-fly fishing. However, if the angler will take the trouble to shorten his terminal tackle somewhat and balance it so that it "turns over" easily, the cast can also be used for dry-fly fishing. The roll cast was first developed to enable an angler to cast his line well out in front of him when there is absolutely no space behind him to allow a back cast. But the roll cast, once learned, has many uses. Modifications of it can be combined with orthodox casting. It is a handy maneuver (see Plates 36 and 37).

On the sand flats of upper Florida Bay, it is a rare day in February, March or April, when the wind is not blowing. Here is a place where the roll cast can be put to excellent use. Many of these flats are dotted with fairly deep pot-holes, and these usually hold their quota of spotted sea trout. Of course they are also liable to be the homes of anything from a half-pound snapper to a 150-pound tarpon. You can never be sure what kind of fish will take your streamer fly when it makes its erratic way across one of these potholes. When the wind is blowing hard—too hard to permit anything like a comfortable back cast—your guide can maneuver the skiff downwind from one pothole to the next while you, standing on the prow, can fish these fascinating spots by roll casting your line ahead of the skiff. It makes for an easy way to fish and saves a great deal of wear and tear on the casting hand.

The fundamentals of the roll cast are as follows. Lay out on the water in front of you about 25 or 30 feet of line. Now, raise your rod tip until it reaches the one o'clock position. For best results, your line should hang straight down from the rod tip to the water beside you. Before the remainder of your line has a chance to sink, bring your rod

Plate 36. A roll cast begins with the rod elevated to the one o'clock position, slightly off the horizontal.

Plate 37. Driving the tip down and through, the senior author shows the completion of a roll cast. This sharp motion brings the line up off the water with a rolling loop out to the target.

forward and down with a decisive slash, throwing in the rod tip at the finish in the direction you wish the cast to go. The line will pick itself up from the water and move away from you in a rolling loop, extending itself straight out before you. Basically, that's all there is to it.

Once you have learned how to roll your line so that it lies out straight at 25 or 30 feet, strip off about 6 or 8 feet of slack from your reel. Now roll out a cast as before, but let go of your slack at the point of release. You will find that it will go along with the cast, shooting out through the guides. With a little experimentation you will discover that you can throw a small or tight loop and a large or wide loop, just as you can throw a tight or wide bow in orthodox casting. The rules are the same. By throwing in the tip at the very completion of the cast—down fairly close to the water—you can throw a small loop. Conversely, by throwing the loop mainly with the middle rod and finishing the cast high—well up from the water—you can throw a surprisingly wide loop. This wide loop is the one that comes in so handy on windy days. The following wind aids the wide loop in its journey forward and allows you to shoot 15 or 20 feet of slack line with the cast.

The Roll Pick-Up

When fishing a dry fly directly upstream or up and slightly across, remember that the current (in common with gravity) is always working against you. Not infrequently your line will drift back to you until it is too close to be picked up in the orthodox way. To regain control the hard way is to strip in slack through the guides until you can make the regular back cast. Then, by using the double shoot, you can work out the slack again until your final forward cast will permit you to extend the line fully. The

Plate 38. The switch pick-up is executed with the rod moving nearly parallel with the water in front of the caster. Slapping the rod tip across from left to right, the caster jumps the line up off the water in a leaping spiral.

easy way in a case like this is to throw a regular roll cast upstream. Then, before the cast has completed itself, pick up the line with the orthodox high back cast and you are back in business with little extra effort or time.

The Switch Pick-Up

An even better pick-up to use when you find that your line is drifting too close to you is the "switch pick-up" (see Plate 38). This pick-up has a dual advantage over the roll pick-up. The cast is a variation of the roll cast, since it makes use of the basic rules of that cast. This is the way you do it.

To execute the switch pick-up, extend the casting hand in front of you with the palm up. With the free-wrist grip, this will place the thumb approximately on top of the rod grip. Now snap the upper rod smartly to the left and slightly upward so that the plane of the rod's motion is 10 or 15 degrees above the horizontal. Be sure to throw in the rod tip sharply at the completion of the sideways motion. With the hand turned into the position described, the free-wrist grip can bring the wrist into full play. If the motion is executed correctly, the line will twist and spiral upward until it has lifted itself from the water. Just before the leader and fly leave the water, execute the orthodox pick-up, throwing the line into the high back cast behind you. The pick-up makes almost no disturbance on the surface of the water and is a great timesaver on a slow-moving pool. Strangely enough, a surprisingly long line can be handled in this way.

Other Variations of the Roll Cast

There are two other variations of the roll cast that have no name but that are extremely useful under certain conditions. For example, suppose you have made your way through the brush and have just stepped into the stream. Your tackle is dry, the dry fly has been freshly oiled, and the line is spooled on the reel. As you look over the stream before proceeding farther, you notice a trout feeding actively over against the far bank. This problem is this—how will you get that freshly oiled fly across 50 feet of water so that it arrives at its destination still dry and "floating on its toes"?

To attempt a regular roll cast means making several casts in the process of working out slack line, and this means wetting the fly in the process. There are two ways to avoid this. One of them is to hold the fly in the left hand, strip line from the reel, working the slack out through the guides by using the regular roll-cast motion, first on the right side, then on the left, alternating as the loop grows, until you have a loop that reaches about halfway to the rising trout. Be sure to execute the final roll of the loop *backhanded* so that your line will be in position to allow a forehanded roll

Plate 39. Finishing a hand-held roll cast, the angler drives the tip down and through, throwing a rolling loop at the target while releasing his fly as the line leaves the water.

cast. Throw this final preparatory loop slightly upstream so that it will drift into position for the final cast.

Now with the loop in position on the water and another loop of slack line in your left hand to be shot through the guides in the final cast, execute the simple, orthodox roll cast, putting into it plenty of extra power. As the loop starts to extend itself, release the fly (see Plate 39). You will find that it will carry to its destination, just upstream from the rising trout. It is almost impossible to illustrate this cast photographically, but if you try it you will find that it works out very well.

Change-of-Direction Cast—First Method

Suppose that the trout to which you have cast has refused the fly on the first drift. You are standing in water, with bushes at your back. The water in front of you is too deep to permit further wading. There is no space for any kind of a back cast, and you have 50 feet of line, leader and fly drifting downstream. Your problem is to pick up that 50 feet of line, leader and fly, dry it in the air, and recast it. With no space for a back cast of any kind, how are you going to do it?

Before attempting to do anything about your line on the water, strip in 2 or 3 loops of slack line and lay them across your left palm, being careful not to let them overlap. Wait until your line has drifted directly downstream from you. Extend the casting hand out in front of you as far as you can (to provide as much clearance as possible from the bushes behind you) and pick up the line with the flat-cast pick-up, either forehand or backhand as the case may be.

Now you can false-cast, back and forth, parallel to the line of the bushes behind you, using care to keep the fly free from those bushes. Work the slack line out through the guides as you false-cast, keeping the last loop of slack in your hand. When you are ready to make the final cast, execute a flat-cast back cast, following through with both your rod tip and your casting arm, lowering the rod tip until it almost touches the water (see Plate 40). As the back cast becomes fully extended, make the forward cast by swinging the rod *up and around toward the target* with a smooth, gradually accelerated motion, finishing with a decisive "throwing in" of the upper rod directly across the stream, at right angles to the line of the false casts (see Plate 41). The line will curl through, following the general path of the rod in its swing, and extend itself across the stream so that the fly once again will drift over the feeding fish. The cast, as stated, is a variation of the roll cast, but the radical change of direction brings out the versatility of the maneuvers of which a fly rod and line are capable.

Change-of-Direction Cast—Second Method

There is another use of the roll-cast principle that is extremely useful. Suppose, for example, you are fishing a fairly wide stream. You have fished out your cast and your line extends directly downstream from you. Out of the corner of your eye you catch the flash of a rising trout to the left and directly across from you near the far bank. Your problem is to pick up your fly from where it is at the moment—directly downstream from you—and place it 4 or 5 feet above the rising trout. First raise your rod tip until the line hangs directly down from it at your side. Now, throw a forehand roll cast (assuming that the flow is from left to right) directly at the far bank, 90 degrees off line. The loop of the roll cast actually will roll out at about 45

degrees. Before the roll cast has completed itself, pick up the line in the orthodox back cast and then swing the forward cast toward the desired spot some few feet above the rising fish. By using this combination roll cast and regular pick-up, you can alter the direction of your cast a full 180 degrees with these relatively few motions. If the cast does not come off exactly as you want it, you can sometimes make a final correction by the use of one false cast, even though you happen to be using a fairly long line at the time.

The Horizontal Cast or Flat Cast

This cast, operating as it does in almost the horizontal plane, is useful in placing your fly or lure under overhanging branches or obstructions. It also serves its purpose when overhead casting is impractical because of overhanging obstructions in your back-cast area. The cast is not difficult but there are a few things you should know about it.

Plate 40. A full arm extension on back cast is mandatory to start a 90-degree change of direction. The back cast follow-through lets the casting arm ride out and slightly down into delivery position.

Plate 41. The rod tip moves forward, up and around in the final delivery of the 90-degree change of direction. The finish of this cast is nothing more than a modified grasshopper. At completion, the tip is driven smartly into the cast, causing the line to loop up and over the target.

The pick-up is made just as you would make the over-head pick-up—gradual acceleration with the final "throwing in" of the upper rod and tip. Move the rod in a plane that is tilted slightly above the horizontal. Put more than necessary power into the pick-up to hold the line above the water where you want it. Again, the forward cast is made in the usual way, aimed a couple of feet above the surface so that the belly of your line will not touch the water, which, inescapably, will cause your fly to "grasshopper" up into trouble. Handled in this way, the line moves forward and back almost in the horizontal plane.

The Galway Cast

This cast was invented by the late F. G. Shaw and named after the Galway River of Great Britain. It is designed to avoid the low bushes or trees that may complicate an ordinary back cast.

To execute the Galway, instead of making the pick-up in the usual way, turn and face the obstructions behind you. Pick up the line with an orthodox forehand cast and toss it high, aiming it to clear the offending shrubbery (see Plate 42). As the line travels to the rear, turn again and cast to your target on the water, this time using the backhand cast. If you care to, you can use forehand casts both front and back, or backhand casts both front and back. It all depends upon the circumstances and how much footwork you want to do (see Plate 43).

The Galway cast can also be used for false casting, either with bushes and trees at your back or in close quarters on a small stream where an unwatched and unaimed back cast can well get you into trouble. By aiming the casts—pick-up, false casts, and final cast—you can save the annoyance of backtracking to retrieve your fly from streamside growth.

Plate 42. Beginning a Galway cast, the angler aims his back cast into a clearing in the foliage behind him. Note that his right foot is forward at this point.

Plate 43. A Galway forward cast involves a full 180-degree turn to the left as the back cast reaches its peak. Hauling sharply with the left hand, the angler speeds up line delivery and makes a normal forward cast, free from obstacles to his rear.

The Wind Cast or Wind Cheater

The back cast is thrown in the usual manner, an effort being made to throw it as high as possible, since the wind tends to knock it down. This cannot be avoided; it is one of the things that you must put up with when fishing in the wind. If you try to throw the cast straight back, the wind will knock it down to the water more often than not. Keep it as high as you can. And don't forget that the wind will shorten your timing somewhat, so make allowance for that. In the forward cast, the rod is slashed smartly down and forward so that the tip nearly touches the water. Throw the upper rod and tip into the cast emphatically at the finish. The line, of course, strikes the water not far from the rod tip, and the cast will roll out "under the wind" until it completes itself (see Plate 44). It is a sloppy method, really a combination of forward cast and roll cast, but it does bring results when other casts do not.

Mending the Cast

When you are fishing a stream, you will often want to cast across a relatively fast current in order to fish a slower feeding run or pocket. If you made such a cast with a straight line, the fly would be whisked out of the far current or the pocket by the intervening fast current. Therefore, to enable you to get a satisfactory drift at the desired spot, you have to "mend your cast."

Suppose, for example, that the current flows from right to left. Directly before you is a fast current and beyond that a slower feeding run. Cast your fly into the far feeding run with the usual orthodox cast. The rod will finish, as usual, almost parallel to the water surface. Now, strip some line from the reel and hold it, as slack line, in your left hand. Next, with the rod tip, throw an upstream curve

Plate 44. A wind cheater is an overdriven forward cast which strikes the water halfway to the target. As it touches down, the power behind the cast drives the upper part of its tight bow in a roll up and over into the wind.

Plate 45. Mending his cast to overcome current drag, the angler flips in an upstream loop to allow the fly a few moments of natural drift.

or "belly" in the line, allowing the slack line to shoot out to form the upstream curve (see Plate 45). The motion is just about the same as that of the roll cast except that it is done horizontally. The rod tip comes up, over and down, and the line near the rod rolls up into an upstream curve. Care should be taken to use only enough power to move the line which comprises the curve itself, allowing the front taper, the leader and the fly, to drift undisturbed. After you have learned the "mend," you will find that you can throw the upstream curve while the cast is completing itself, even before the fly has touched the water.

The Overcast

This is an extremely useful cast to use either with the wet fly or the dry fly. Suppose you have seen a good trout swing behind your wet fly as it moves across a pocket or a feeding run. Since the fly was not moving naturally, the trout merely came up for a close look, but refused to take. If wading depth permits, move to a spot directly upstream from the spot where you saw the fish. Now, work out line until you can reach slightly beyond your target. Aim your final cast high so that you can check it in midair directly above or slightly beyond your target; then raise the rod tip and allow the line and fly to settle to the surface slightly upstream from the location of the fish. By doing so, you will provide enough slack line to enable you to drift your fly down to the fish in a natural manner.

With a dry fly, the overcast is a fine way to fish pockets in a riffle with a short line. If you use a well-oiled, bushy fly, you can overcast the pocket. Raise the rod tip rather smartly as the fly nears the surface, causing the fly to come toward you at a 45-degree angle. As the fly strikes the water, it will skip once or twice before coming to rest. This overcast with the dry fly is also called "the bump cast."

There are other casts, combinations of various well-defined casts, which you will develop as your technique improves. For example, when you are fishing in a cross wind that is blowing from right to left, it is wise, as a matter of safety, to pick up your line with a backhand back cast. This will keep you clear of sharp hook points. As the line travels rearward, the wind carries it well to the left. It is then possible to execute the forward cast forehanded, since in this way you can apply more power. Every good angler has some of these little tricks up his sleeve, and it is this inside knowledge, born of experience, that makes fly casting such a fascinating sport.

BASS-BUG CASTING 8

UNFORTUNATELY, all too many people regard bass-bug fishing as a stepchild of trout-fly casting. You see these fellows on bass lakes and rivers attempting to make do with a trout rod. To consider bass-bug fishing in this light is a serious error. To fish a bass bug and fish it well, you need the finest tackle that money can buy, specially designed for the job. With the possible exception of casting to a feeding bonefish on a shallow sand flat, bass-bug fishing is the most exacting form of fly fishing, since it places decided emphasis on both distance and accuracy. Bass—and this is particularly true of big, adult bass—will not stand crowding. To fish a bass bug successfully, you should be able to do so at distances of 65 feet and better, all day long. You must also be able to place the bug accurately, exactly where you want it, cast after cast. This is not easy to learn. It stands to reason that for a job of this magnitude you must have the absolute tops in tackle. No doubt about it—bass-bug fishing separates the men from the boys in very short order.

Although bass-bug fishing is usually done from a boat, it is best to learn and practice bass-bug casting on dry land,

114

keeping in mind that this type of casting is done either sitting or standing. Perhaps the best way to start is to sit on a chair or a piano stool set out on the lawn or in some other open space. Using a regular tournament target, a hula hoop or an old bicycle tire, learn to handle your bass-bug gear just as though you were seated in a canoe.

You should begin to practice at reasonably short ranges, say 40 feet. Rig your tackle just as though you were fishing —line, leader and hookless bug. Try using various types of bugs, some with low air resistance and others with more weight and higher air resistance. Place your target so that you can learn to cast with the wind, against the wind, and across the wind. After practicing while seated, put in more practice while standing, until you are proficient in casting from either position. When you reach the point where you can place that bug in the target 4 out of 5 times running, at distances of 60 or more feet, you are ready to go bass-bug fishing.

As explained in Chapter 2, a bass-bug rod is large as fly rods go—at least 9 feet and preferably 9 feet 6 inches. This rod requires a fairly large reel and a torpedo-head or forward-taper line. A bass bug is much heavier and bulkier than a trout fly, and its bulk sets up wind resistance. You *must* have stout tackle to handle such a lure. So before you attempt any bass-bug fishing, make up your mind that you must outfit yourself properly.

To handle bass bug well, you should know all of the orthodox casts and the special casts. Most of the time you will need only the regular forehand pick-up, back cast, and forward cast. But bass water usually is big water and as a rule you have little or no protection from the wind. On windy days, you will often find that orthodox methods are not practical. You should therefore know every trick in the bag and master *all* of the casts before you go bass-bug fishing.

As stated, bass-bug fishing consists of accuracy casting at long ranges with comparatively heavy gear. This means that the greatest amount of your casting will be done with the rod moving in a plane that is only slightly off the perpendicular. By keeping your rod in this upright position, you reduce the probability of errors. Should you overcast or apply too much power, the bug—at the completion of the cast—will not snap around into a curve, as it will if you hold your rod slightly slantwise. Instead, it will roll out and over, arriving at the target too fast perhaps, but at least free of entanglements with bushes or water growth at either side of the pocket.

Bass-bug fishing, as you probably know, is nearly always done along a shore line. This naturally means that you will be contending with overhanging branches and brush a good share of the time. Bass, the contrary creatures, like to lie *under* such obstructions, not beside them. It is your job to get that bug under there, right on the big boy's plate. To attempt to do this with a flat cast while using such a long line is courting destruction. More often than not, the line will touch the water before the bug has reached its destination. Immediately, the bug will "grasshopper" up and over, usually to become entangled with the overhang which you are trying to avoid. To enable you to place your bug in such difficult spots safely and consistently, a special cast—the overhand positive curve cast—has been developed.

The Overhand Positive Curve Cast

The pick-up is made in the usual way, a regular forehand pick-up, throwing the line into the usual high back cast

Plate 46. The overhand positive curve cast is one of the handiest tricks in your bag. Throw in the tip of the rod sharply as you turn the palm of your casting hand toward you during the finish of the cast. The line will snap around to the left at the completion of the cast, parallel with the water.

with the rod moving through a plane only slightly off the vertical. Start the forward cast in the usual way until you reach the point where normally you would apply the final flip or throwing-in of the upper rod to complete the cast. At this point the cast differs from the regular forward cast in which you throw in the tip with the palm facing the direction of the cast. Instead of throwing in the upper rod and the tip in the usual manner, roll your wrist sharply outward as you complete the cast. This will turn the palm of your hand so that it is facing you at the completion of the cast instead of facing the direction of the cast.

By rolling the wrist and turning the palm toward you as you complete the cast, the upper rod and tip will move through a half circle to the right. The bow in the line, instead of moving out, up, and over in an almost vertical plane, will actually move forward in a plane parallel to the water (see Plate 46). As the cast completes itself, the leader and bug will snap around to the left, in this way placing the bug well under the overhanging obstructions. It is an extremely useful cast, one which every bass-bug fisherman should know and know thoroughly.

Bass-Bug Casting Tips

All bass bugs have more weight and greater air resistance than the average trout fly. To complicate matters, no two patterns weigh the same nor do they have the same air resistance. Some bugs with low air resistance (such as the famous Wilder-Dilg Bug) cast easily and turn over rather sharply at the completion of the cast. Others, notably the "popper" types, require more effort to turn over at the end of a cast.

To compensate for this variation in casting performance, you can adjust your leader weight and length. Generally, it is wise to use about 10 feet of leader, tapered to a 6-pound or 8-pound point. To compensate for the extra air resistance of some bugs, it may be necessary to drop back to a 10-pound or 12-pound point and reduce the leader length to 7 or 8 feet. A little experimenting will give you the answer. Cut back gradually until you arrive at the proper bug-leader balance.

As mentioned earlier, bass-bug fishing is an accuracy job at long ranges. It is for that reason that your rod should move almost through a vertical plane. But there is a trick in "sighting your cast" when you are bass-bug fishing that is a definite aid to accuracy.

Before you pick up a fished-out cast, point your rod tip

at your next target. Make your pick-up in the usual way. As you bring the rod through in the forward cast, forget about rod, line and bug. Move your forearm and hand *directly* in line with that target, the palm of the hand facing the target *directly* as you complete the cast. This motion automatically keeps your rod exactly in line and thus moves your line, leader and bug to the desired destination.

Line handling in bass-bug casting from a boat is not at all complicated. All you need to do is to strip in the slack line and allow it to coil in the bottom of the boat. If you are wearing shoes with laces, untie the bowknot and tie the laces *behind* your ankles. If they are not long enough, stuff them into the sides of your shoes. If you don't do this, your line coils are inevitably bound to become entangled in the bows of your shoe laces. And once your slack line is coiled at your feet, *don't move your feet.* If you do, you will step on a coil or two. Not only does this tend to ruin the finish of your line; it will also spoil your next cast.

Most men stand up in a bass-bug boat. This is all right if you have a good sense of balance. But you must remember *never* to shift your weight as you cast. If you do, you can very easily lose your balance, and that is a fine way to take an impromptu bath, not to mention possible loss of expensive tackle. Also, a shift of weight will create ripples on the quiet surface. These constitute a warning to the bass that all is not as it should be. You should set your feet so that your weight is evenly distributed, and then anchor yourself in that position.

Bass-bug fishing is not always done from a boat. Sometimes you will find a lake with a hard sand bottom. Then you can put on your waders and fish ahead of you as you make your way slowly through the shallows. Again, many good smallmouthed rivers consist of a series of riffles and wadable pools. A boat in this sort of river is a nuisance. Best wear wading gear and depend upon your legs for transportation.

Wading raises both casting and line-handling problems. Since you are waist deep in water, the business of keeping your back cast high and clear of the water surface behind you requires more effort on the back cast than you would normally use. But it pays to exert this extra effort, since a sloppy back cast surely does not help your accuracy.

Handling your slack line while wading depends upon where you are wading. In a lake, there usually are reeds growing in the shallows. Thus, your best bet is to collect your slack line in loops that you can lay across the palm of your left hand. In a river, the current will carry your

Plate 47. Streaming loose slack down with the current, the angler plays his bug while he moves into position for the next cast. With today's floating lines, this momentary immersion of the line does no harm and keeps it out of casting way.

slack line downstream from you if you simply strip it in and allow it to fall in the water beside you (see Plate 47). This is the easy way to handle slack in a river, but if you prefer loops, by all means use them.

When casting in a river, it is always a good plan to let the current help you when you are playing your bug. Instead of casting directly across-current, causing the flow to put a bow in your line and pull it under, cast down and across on about a 45-degree angle. This enables you to keep a tight line on your bug at all times. Also, the current will flow under your line, keeping it on the surface so that the pick-up is easy after the cast has been fished out.

One last caution when you are fishing a shore line in a river: you will often be placing the bug in backwater pockets, inside the current. If you "mend" your cast, throwing an upstream loop as the bug lands, you can fish the bug across the pocket so that it moves in a natural way. If you cast directly into the pocket without throwing the upstream loop, the current will cause the bug to drag out in an unnatural way, thereby ruining the cast.

SALT-WATER FLY CASTING 9

To look at the Florida Keys today—a maze of motels, restaurants and other civilized refinements—few would believe that this was a desolate region until 1947, when the current craze of using a fly rod in salt water was born. The discovery that some 38 species of salt-water game fish would take fly-rod lures had the same impact on this once mangrove-ridden area that the discovery of gold had on California.

Salt-water fly fishing began with the bonefish, that gray speedster of the sand flats in Florida Bay. It started with hastily adapted fresh-water tackle which soon proved to be ill-suited to the task at hand. There were a few of us in at the beginning in those halcyon days of no outboard traffic and many fish within easy running distance. They were truly happy days, even if guides rusted off rods within the space of a week and ferrules locked with corrosion overnight if the tackle was not thoroughly washed down in fresh water at the end of the day to remove the virulent salt incrustations that threatened the moving parts of rods and reels alike.

During that first year, we started with a battery of oversized bamboo bass rods ranging from 9 to 10 feet in length. At the end of that first span of months, we had broken over half of them, put better-than-permanent sets in the remainder, and spent countless hours repairing tackle—rods and reels alike. In doing so, we landed fish; to be sure, only a small percentage of what we managed to hook. The unofficial fly-rod tarpon record crept slowly upward from 47 pounds to a whopping 66 pounds. Then, and only then did the tackle manufacturers learn what we needed and start to produce proper equipment, though some were still reluctant to admit that salt-water fly casting was little more than a passing fad.

There is a momentary feeling of helplessness that converts an angler to a shaking shell of his former self when he lengthens line to cast at a tarpon fully as long as he is tall. The explosive crash of a 15-pound snook in the still water of a mangrove pocket causes the heart to leap in sheer shock. The swift overtaking of a streamer by a bone-fish in that instant before the line tightens is enough in itself to transform an experienced man into a rank novice. In short, salt-water fly casting is scarcely a fad or a craze, but a separate division of fly-rod sport that is equal to any other and superior to most.

Salt-water tackle is a means to an end where delicacy of cast is demanded with some species and sheer rod strength (which transforms a fly rod into a killing instrument capable of handling fish far larger than one might expect) in others. Over the past decade, radical approaches have been tried and have proved to be satisfactory when applied to their own particular function in the amazing complexity of the sport itself. How else would the brute-like "flat rod" have been developed—a rod with a sensitive hooking tip, a powerful middle section, and a butt capable of stopping a charging tarpon or a bank-bound snook? In this one refinement the rod ceases to be the contemplative instrument we associate with streams and lakes and becomes a weapon capable of subduing anything you are fortunate enough to hook and strong enough to whip.

If salt-water fly casting was as exacting in precision as dry-fly fishing, not five men in the country could handle the tackle. With the possible exception of canal fishing for snook and tarpon in the southern back country, the sport gives the angler a tremendous amount of latitude in accuracy. Even bonefishing, which was launched with the greatest "hard sell" of difficulty with which any sport was ever foisted on the angling public, is relatively easy on the angler and allows far greater tolerance for mistakes than does spotting a dry fly over a feeding trout in a riffle pocket during the course of a fluttering downstream wind. In short, you have all outdoors in which to heave your lure, and if you must define or separate the sport in terms of casting, you have but to arrive at the decision in your own mind as to *how* you want to present the lure rather than *where*.

As it was in the beginning for us (armed with equipment far too inadequate for the task), the first major hazard any new salt-water fly caster encounters is the constant presence of wind. It blows every day on the flats—on some days at a modest 5 knots; on others as a raging gale. To fish under such conditions, you must learn to make do—to let the very thing that could ruin your day work for you. Wind is always a nuisance, but it can and must be handled if you are to spend happy hours on the sand flats.

How to Handle Wind

In earlier chapters we have emphasized the axiom that a high back cast is the beginning of a perfect forward cast. As with every rule, there is an exception—here, it is your position in relation to the wind direction.

The perfect setup for any cast—in both fresh and salt water—is to have the wind quartering from your rear on the noncasting side. This allows you to make such drift compensation as you require to hit your target while not endangering your own anatomy or that of your fishing companions. In salt-water casting, where 3/0 hook sizes are average, this becomes exceedingly important. Let's examine this problem of wind in detail.

(1) *Casting into a head wind*——Your back cast is thrown back with the bow as high as you can aim it. Wind plus gravity will knock it down in a hurry, and since a high back cast will result in a sharp, tight forward bow, concentrate on this even if you must turn your head and watch it. As your back cast levels off, apply power evenly to near completion and then drive the tip down and through, tightening your forward bow to the extreme and punching the cast in low under the wind to the target.

(2) *Wind on the casting quarter*——Perhaps the most dangerous of all casts, particularly in a heavy wind, this position requires skill on your part. It can be handled in two ways, either forehand or backhand. As we have stressed the necessity of your learning to cast one-handed through a full 180 degrees, it is simpler (and far safer) to take this cast off the water and return it from the backhand position (see Plate 48).

With the palm of the casting hand facing your target, lift the line sharply with the full rod, throwing back a

Plate 48. Casting in a crosswind with a big rod can be dangerous unless you handle the line on the off or downwind side as demonstrated here. Remember to compensate for wind drift by casting to the right or left of your target, according to wind direction.

Plate 49. Having a downwind cast with a "flat rod," the angler uses the *middle rod on delivery*, allowing the tip to follow through of itself, while the resulting wide bow carries his cast long and high.

normal high back cast over your left shoulder. At back-cast completion, bring your rod through on a normal plane, remembering to cast to the *right* of your target to compensate for wind drift. The forward cast requires a normal bow and should be held a shade higher to allow the wind to push it out there for you.

(3) *Using a following wind*——Here is where the exception defies the rule—a high back cast is what you do not need. Raise the cast from the water and exaggerate your follow-through, dropping the line far lower than usual. On your forward cast, use the middle rod only, allowing the bow to balloon out high and wide so that the wind acts as your ally (see Plate 49). With a single haul on pick-up, you can heave 75 feet of line with little effort, letting the wind and the middle rod do most of the labor for you, and shooting most of the cast out through the guides as the wind takes the line away from you.

(4) *Wind on the off-casting quarter*——This is nearly an optimum wind position and is handled in normal back- and forward-casting fashion, except to make allowance for wind drift. Remember to make one short false cast here to learn about how much you must allow for wind drift, and then aim your cast a corresponding distance to the *left* of your target.

With the exception of blind-casting potholes and channels, a great majority of the casting done in salt water is for cruising fish, many of these fast-moving "coasters" skulking in and out of the deep water to feed on the run over the shallow flats. Of all the species you may catch on a fly, only four will give you a visual sighting indication in advance. The redfish, the bonefish and the permit will either "mud" (through their rooting efforts they throw out a muddy patch of water downtide from their position) or "tail" (stick part of the body out of the water as they tip up to feed in the shallows). The tarpon will "bibble" (lie dormant just under the surface with his dorsal fin and tail tip projecting above the water), thus giving you a fair-timed shot at him. The remainder are a sight-aim-cast proposition, with the first cast the most important one of the lot.

The Drive Cast

The drive cast was developed by people like us whose hands tired from casting to and fighting big fish all day long. By midafternoon, a hard, punched-in bow at some 60 feet or better is wearing on the casting hand and fore-arm when you are swinging a 7-ounce-plus "flat rod" loaded down with a big reel and a torpedo-head line.

About all there is to a drive cast is a compensating hand turn at the top of your back-cast follow-through (see Plate 50). Rather than bring the hand through with the conventional free-wrist grip to deliver it on target line, you slide your grip over on *top* of the rod, letting the thumb of your casting hand become the fulcrum against which the lever of the big rod must work (see Plate 51).

We stress here that the hand grip must shift at the end of the back-cast follow-through, for one major reason—the free-wrist grip makes it far easier for anyone but the professional caster to throw a perfect back cast. Once this operation is completed, however, the slight hand shift to bring the thumb into the driving position of the forward delivery adds impetus to your cast while minimizing effort on your part (see Plate 52).

As with any other casting sequence, the drive cast is aimed on a vertical-rod plane of movement. To be sure, wind will have an effect on rod angle of delivery, but aside from wind compensation, the basic cast remains the same with but one more minor adjustment. All drive casts are thrown with a tight bow, necessitating the application of heavy tip action at the very end of the cast to punch your cast in low and hard to the cruising target of your choice. By doing this, you reduce mistakes in wind compensation and make your first cast count where a loosely executed sequence probably would cost you a crack at a possible prize fish.

The Importance of Slack

Until you hook your first fish in salt water, you have yet to believe the tremendous explosive drive these fish have as compared to fresh-water species. A tarpon's rampaging run is an awesome thing to behold; a bonefish will have you on backing without your ever being conscious of the departure of your casting line (this being 120 feet in length in the average GAF line). Therefore, the number of fish you land and the amount of tackle you *do not* break up is in direct proportion to the care you take in handling your slack line.

As you start your first drift down a flat, lay out 70 feet of line and then coil it loosely and *evenly* between your feet (be sure you remember to tie your shoelaces around your ankles). If you do not have a cast at a fish within the first five minutes of poling, recast out the slack and recoil it once more with care. Keep this up until you hook a fish, and you will find that it pays dividends.

This is not a book dedicated to fishing method but rather one devoted exclusively to casting method. However, it would not fulfill its purpose without a few words that may seem to infringe on the former. Keep these rules firmly in mind and you will land far more fish than you lose. When

←

Plate 50. The drive cast starts with a full arm follow-through on the back cast. The left hand is still completing the single haul stage of the lift-off in this picture while the angler watches his back cast ride out high.

→

Plate 51. The hand turn in the drive cast—placing the thumb directly on top of the rod grip and behind the cast for additional leverage—is implemented by the second-stage haul of the left hand to build up forward cast momentum.

→

Plate 52. Driving over and through, the angler finishes the second-stage haul as he applies full rod power to the finish of the drive cast. Not pretty to watch, but deadly in effect, this cast has proved itself both in salt-water and bass-bug casting.

you complete your cast to your fish, watch your slack, not the fish (see Plates 53, 54 and 55). Fix your eyes between your feet and lay those coils evenly as you retrieve. Don't worry about the fish. He will make his presence very firmly known on strike.

When you feel the line tighten on strike, *pull* the hook home and then concentrate once more on your slack. Until you have that fish on the reel, you stand an excellent chance

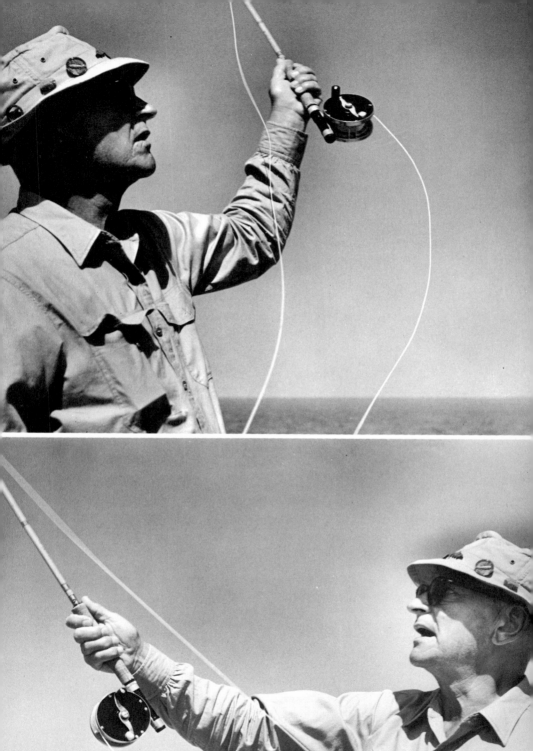

Plate 53. Salt-water slack handling involves a good deal of care with your coils. Retrieve through the thumb and second finger of your casting hand, placing each coil carefully on the floor of the skiff.

↗

Plate 54. Leaning forward to watch his coils, the angler ignores his quarry as he places his slack carefully. Once having hooked his fish, the angler must have his slack leave the rod "clean" to avoid disastrous tackle break-up.

→

Plate 55. Handling slack on a slam-bang run is a touchy job. Here, the angler makes a shooting guide out of his left thumb and forefinger to iron out loops as they jump off the floor of the skiff.

of having your slack jump into a balled-up coil that will break you up so fast you will never know what hit you. As the fish makes his break for deep water, make a definite, oversized guide out of your left hand, locking the tips of the thumb and forefinger together to lead the slack coils up off the floor of the skiff through your rod and out to the fish. As the last of the slack clears the skiff and the fish is on the drag of your reel, you can congratulate yourself on having a job behind you—well done.

The Lock Position

As in every collaboration, the authors do not always agree on all points brought forward. In the case of father and son, this can lead to a discussion of some heat. Rather than start a family feud over the matter, we show you here (see Plates 56 and 57) our two versions of the lock position used to handle oversized salt-water species when they are in full, rampaging flight. Both are correct in every detail; they differ only in individual preference rather than in general usefulness.

The senior author prefers the lock position at belt level, placing the palm of his left hand behind the reel seat and bracing his forearm against his left hip. This, combined with a full reach up the rod with the right hand, gives him heavy leverage against any large fish.

The junior author has his own version of the lock. He braces the reel in the same manner as the senior author, but rather than set down into the lock with his forearm, he puts the elbow of his left arm inside the left hip and reaches up the rod as far as his right arm will go. This allows him to lock, as well as lean, back into the rod to lay heavy pressure against an off-running fish.

Plate 56. One version of the salt-water lock position is demonstrated by the senior author. The butt of the rod is placed against the belt buckle, with the right hand low on the grip. The left hand rides up the rod to apply extra leverage against the fish.

Plate 57. In full lock, the junior author prefers to brace his left elbow against his belt, left palm behind the reel, while his right arm rides up the rod almost to the first guide to apply heavy pressure against a hooked fish.

Both authors, however, are in firm agreement on this one point—salt-water fishing is not a gentle sport (see Plate 58). We feel that the *longer* you have a fish on before bringing him to gaff or net, the better chance you stand of losing him. If you are to bear down on the fish, lay back on him until you are giving yourself as much if not more abuse than you are giving him; you will either land him far faster than you dreamed possible or you will lose him if he is lightly or poorly hooked, and be able to start your search for another without wasting precious minutes. While this theory may sound radical, it has proved to be sound and has netted us both many good fish in far less time than one might expect it would take normally.

Beating the Mangrove Nightmare

A mangrove bush is a built-in lure grabber, common to tropical salt water, that—until you learn to beat it—can ruin more days of fishing for you than any other hazard you will encounter (see Plate 59). Dense, green, shade-providing and rubbery in texture, it makes lovely cover for snook and other species, as well as presenting a casting problem of major magnitude.

Not all salt-water fly casting is done from a skiff; there are inland salt-water lakes and canals which are loaded to capacity with such scrappers as baby tarpon and snook. In the early days, several of us knew of such gold mines, and kept them to ourselves for many years before they became common knowledge. All were overgrown with mangroves, and therein lay the rub. These hot spots, not being wadable, were fished from the bank, the casting being done *between* the mangrove bushes.

In the chapter on bass-bug casting, we spoke of the use of the overhand positive curve cast, a gem of a delivery we

Plate 58. Rod overhead, the senior author stems the first run of a bonefish. Using this position, he is able to cut down on skin friction as well as keep his line free of bottom obstructions.

Plate 59. A caster's nightmare is an overhung mangrove pocket where tarpon and snook lie back in the shade.

developed under pure stress of necessity. To our definite knowledge, this is the only cast that can whip a mangrove-overhung pocket. If you plan on doing any canal, lake or back-country fishing in the mangrove regions, practice this cast until you have it down pat. It will save you many a headache.

One more tip will eliminate many a bad cast. Before throwing *any* cast at a mangrove pocket, premeasure your cast with a false cast just this side of your target. Allow just enough "shoot" on final delivery to spot your lure exactly and accurately instead of casting it on a guess-and-hope basis. Practice alone will save you many a lure. Learn the overhand positive curve and put it, plus some common sense, to use, and those mangrove bushes will cease to bother you.

ROD ACTION 10

ROD action is a nebulous thing. It is probably best described as the "feel" of a fly rod as it flexes in your hand, either in actual casting or in a tackleshop when you are looking over new rods. Just about every fly-rod man will speak learnedly of rod action, but relatively few know much about it. It is like the wheeze you hear in art galleries: "I don't know much about art, but I know what I *like.*" The same applies to fly rods and rod action. Some self-styled experts will prate about rod action endlessly. "Why," they say, "with that little seven-foot-six top-action job, I can lay out a hundred feet, easy." The truth of the matter is that this feat is neither easy nor—in most circumstances—necessary.

When the world's female professional casting champion, Joan Salvato, who knows thousands of casters, was asked how many men she knew who could cast 100 feet with orthodox fly-rod tackle, her answer was: "About five, and then I wouldn't be sure."

Satisfactory action in a fly rod means that you have a rod, the bending of which will lay out a fly line accurately and comfortably, just where you want that line to go, at reasonable fishing distances of—say—30 to 70 feet. You don't need or want a powerhouse for fishing. Seldom, if ever, do you need to cast outside the 30- to 70-foot range. That being the case, use a rod that will be *comfortable* and that will not overwork your casting hand.

Rod actions vary pretty much with the caster. Some men like fast rods and some prefer slow ones. It all depends on the caster and his preferences.

By and large, the idea that a dry-fly rod must be a fast-action job and that a wet-fly rod should be limp and slow has been fairly well discarded. With our trout rods of today, you can handle dry fly or wet fly equally well.

A good many men, when they are looking over new rods, assemble the rod, hold it by the grip, and then shake or wobble it, nodding approval or lack of it as they do so. From this motion only one possible thing can be learned. By wobbling a rod, you set up a vibrational node in the upper rod, the tip moving one way and the middle and lower rod in the opposite direction. If this vibrational node is relatively close to the tip guide, you can be fairly sure that the rod is of the top-action variety. Conversely, if the node is fairly well down toward the middle rod, the proba-bilities are that you have a fairly slow rod, with the action distributed throughout the entire rod. Neither of these bits of information are conclusive or accurate. You can't tell much by wobbling.

As explained in Chapter 2, to find out what kind of action is in a rod you should hold the rod by the grip, directly in front of you (see Plate 11). Use both hands if you wish; that way you can hold the rod grip more rigidly. Now start moving the rod tip back and forth in a horizontal plane. Looking along the length of the rod as it bends, you can see exactly *where* it bends, how the action distributes itself along the rod. In other words, this method will give you the "action picture" of the rod.

There are several distinct types of rod action. First, there is the top-action job. As the rod flexes, you will note that most of the bending occurs in the upper two thirds of the rod. Usually the tip is quite soft, showing a rather exaggerated bending as you increase the arc of the rod's motion, back and forth. If you like these rods, that's your privilege. Our advice, however, is to shun them as you would the plague.

Then there is the "circular" or uniform action or taper. As you flex this type of rod, you will note that the bending is actually uniform. Of course, the upper rod does bend slightly more than the part directly above the grip, but there is no place along the entire length of the rod that bends noticeably more, proportionately, than other parts of the rod.

The development of the parabolic rod action has an interesting story behind it. Charles Ritz of the Ritz Hotel in Paris planned to go fishing in the Bavarian Alps with a party of anglers. The day before he was scheduled to start on this trip, he went to the factory of Pizon and Michel in Paris, and selected a rod to his liking, an 8-foot rod. Wishing to have some last-minute work done on the rod, he left it in the factory, with instructions to have it delivered at the hotel early the next morning.

The rod was a two-piece affair. To save carrying space, the factory had set up the two sections so that the rod grip was separate, the bottom end of the lower section being equipped with a ferrule that fitted into the top of the grip. Since the factory did not have on hand a rigid metal case which fitted it, they sent it over in a cloth case. It was delivered by a boy who was riding a bicycle.

During the ride from factory to hotel, the boy allowed the end of the cloth rod case to become caught between the spokes of the front wheel and the bicycle frame. The youngster ripped out a couple of spokes of the wheel and took a good tumble in doing so. He said nothing of this mishap to Charley. He simply handed him the rod and departed.

Ill-advisedly, Charley did not take a spare rod with him on the trip. The four men in the group were crowded into a small French car, and space was at a premium. Arriving at camp, Charley found that both of the rod sections were broken—the tip had lost 3 inches, as had the lower end of the lower section. Strangely enough, there were no spare rods in the party, so Charley had to make do with what was left of his new rod.

Using what materials were on hand, he managed to set the tip guide on one end and the base ferrule on the other. This left him with a rod that was about 7 feet 6 inches. Curious to see how his camp repairs had worked out, he strung a line on the rod and took it down to the stream. Charley is a good caster, a tournament caster. He found that by adjusting his timing he could actually use the rod in his fishing. But the rod had a strange action indeed. Most of the bending was done in the lower one third of the rod, the upper two thirds functioning as a lever. But Charley also noticed that the upper two thirds, acting as a lever, delivered *all* of the power of the cast to the line at the point of release with almost no follow-through. The result was that he could cast a perfectly straight line with it at surprising distances. The effect of this accident was not felt in the casting field for several years. It was not until after Ritz and the senior author experimented in the mid-thirties that the Payne Parabolic was born. Following this came the work of Everett Garrison, a talented custom rodmaker, whose modification of the original harsh parabolic action brought about the semiparabolic rod, easily the most pleasant casting instrument ever devised.

The semiparabolic rod action is, without question, the ideal action for light trout rods. In view of the fact that the whole rod is put to work on almost all lengths of casts, a light rod is thereby endowed with a disproportionate amount of power for its weight. The timing of this taper is somewhat slower than that of other actions and is some-thing to which the caster must accustom himself. But once you have learned to accept this slight change of timing, you will find this rod a delight to use on any trout stream. The comparatively slow, comfortable action actually does most of the casting for you.

Conversely, unless you have an unusually strong casting hand, semiparabolic action is not suited to the bass-bug rod. In the 9-foot-6-length, it requires much effort to put a semiparabolic bass-bug rod to work for you. For bass-bug casting, best stick to the uniform taper, distributed through-out the entire rod, and avoid anything savoring of fast action for handling a bass bug. A long, slow rod in uni-form action will not only ease the strain on your casting hand, but is also far more accurate than a fast rod.

For the bonefish flats, where accuracy and distance pay off, the 9-foot-6 rod with semiparabolic action, either in bamboo or glass, is ideal. This action is strong enough to provide ample power for the average casting hand and slow enough to insure accuracy. Usually, a cast to a feeding bonefish is a one-cast affair. If you cast too far away, the fish won't see it, and if you cast too close, he will flush. The extra strain that the semiparabolic rod places on the casting hand is not oppressive in view of the fact that casting is not continuous. You cast only after you have stalked the fish and the guide has placed the skiff in position for the try. Conversely, for "blind-casting" the potholes on a sand flat, the 9-foot-6 rod in uniform action is preferable to the semiparabolic. Actually, a good bass-bug rod is ideal for this job.

For the "flat rod," the big heavy-duty weapon that will subdue those big game fish that inhabit salt water, the rules are slightly different. For this sort of fishing, a stout butt joint is an absolute *must*. When you hold the rod in the lock position while playing a going-away fish, you should be able to grasp the butt joint with your arm fully extended, and to do so with safety, at least midway up the lower section. This is no job for bamboo, but glass stands up very well under such treatment.

This means, of course, that your "flat rod" will, unavoidably, be of the top-action variety to a certain degree. It should be of "circular" or uniform taper, and the action should come down into the butt joint as far as possible, considering the requirements. If you will look at the pictures of Joan Salvato in action, you will see what can be done with a "flat rod." Joan borrowed this rod from us to do that casting series. With enough line load, a good "flat rod" actually can be put to work clear down to the rod grip.

The Vibration Theory

Some anglers, and regrettably, some factories, feel that satisfactory rod actions can be determined by vibrations. With the rod grip or reel seat held immovable, the rod is vibrated up and down with the tip of the index finger, the rod being allowed to set its own timing. The number of vibrations per minute determines the quality of the rod as a casting tool. The reasoning behind this theory is just about as fallacious as anything can be.

What you actually get when you vibrate a rod in this manner is pendulum action, pure and simple—weight times length. Any fly rod that is built anywhere within reasonable semblance of a usable rod will, at a certain length, vibrate approximately the same as another fly rod of the same length, regardless of taper and action.

For example, four 8-foot fly rods were vibrated and the vibrations carefully counted. Deliberately, four rods of radically different tapers and action were used. There was a glass rod of uniform taper: a Leonard of the Hewitt steep-taper design; a Winston that is a compromise between uniform action and semiparabolic action; and a Garrison of pure semiparabolic action (in reality the "eighth rod" that gave Garrison the clue to this action many years ago). Here is the score:

Glass, uniform action	128 vibrations per minute
Winston semipar uniform	130 vibrations per minute
Hewitt steep taper	130 vibrations per minute
Garrison semipar	132 vibrations per minute

As you can see, vibrations don't tell you a great deal about rod action. In view of the fact that some factories allow a margin for error of about 12 vibrations per minute, you can see that the whole theory is off base.

Fly-rod action is indeed complex, for it depends on the law governing the flexibility coefficient of a flexible rod which *varies as the cube of the diameter*. This being the case, a variation of as little as a thousandth of an inch in the diameter of a rod section can make a great deal of difference in the way the rod will behave in use.

It is this extremely sensitive formula that gives bamboo the edge over glass when it comes to setting up high-grade fly rods. Bamboo rod sections can be taken to the work-bench and the action planed in with scraper or sand block. With a glass rod section, the action must be built in as the section is assembled. Once the section is put together and the plastic coagulant or binder applied, that section is finished as far as action is concerned. Perhaps the rod companies can solve this difficult problem with glass rods, but so far they have not been able to arrive at an entirely satisfactory solution.

LENGTHENING THE CAST | 11

As we have indicated, in your actual fishing you will rarely find that you need more than 65 or 70 feet of line, leader and fly. But now and again when you are fishing big water, you need to stretch your cast up to 90 feet or so.

To demonstrate the long cast or power cast, we borrowed Joan Salvato from Dick Wolff, Vice-President of the Garcia Corporation, with which she is signed up as one of its exhibition casters. Joan is the world's female professional casting champion (see Plate 60). She dominates this field just as the immortal Babe Didrikson used to dominate female track and golf.

Joan started tournament casting when she was eleven years old under the tutelage of her father, Jim Salvato, who has been interested in tournament casting just about all of his life. When Joan was eighteen, Bill Taylor of Paterson, New Jersey—a good tournament caster in his own right—took her under his wing. She soon began to win fly-rod distance events in tournaments. From 1943 to 1951, she won at least one amateur title each year in the national tournament held under the direction of the National Association of Anglers and Casting Clubs.

The year 1951 was Joan's banner year. In this one year she won six national titles including the open fishermen's fly-rod event—pros and amateurs, men and women. She was the only girl, casting against 15 or 20 of the world's best casters, and she beat the late Johnny Dieckman, world champion, by 1/3 of a foot average in the fly-rod distance.

In 1948, she competed in the International Casting Tournament (the first to be held after World War II) in London. In this tournament she won first place in the open 5/8-ounce accuracy plug event and second place in the open 1/4-ounce plug event. Her longest distance cast in the "trout-fly" fly-rod event in competition is 161 feet. These statistics and achievements will give you some idea of what this girl can do with fishing tackle.

Joan is now married, the mother of two children, and lives in South Miami. In response to a telephone call, she drove down to the Florida Keys, bringing her distance fly-rod line, some borrowed rods and a casting target.

Our photographs were taken at a friend's swimming pool, put at our disposal for the occasion. In the interests of good photography, it was necessary for Joan to cast toward the sun. This meant that she was casting into a brisk east wind, about 20 knots or so. She stood on the masonwork wall at the end of the pool, and with a borrowed rod (our "flat rod") she threw a measured cast into that wind 128 feet. There are not five *men* in the world who can duplicate that performance, and it is doubtful that *any* woman can.

Joan has small hands, wrists and arms. Indeed, the average man can encircle her wrist with thumb and index finger. To enable her to pick up that heavy distance line, she and

Bill Taylor have evolved a special way to grip a fly rod so that she could compensate for her small hands and forearms. After all, Joan is not a big girl; she weighs about 115 pounds with an unabridged Webster's Dictionary tucked under her arm. If you study the photographs, you will note that she holds the rod grip so that the reel seat is braced firmly against her wrist and forearm, making rod, hand and forearm practically a solid unit. This enables her to put the strength of her arm, as well as her hand, into the pick-up of the heavy tournament line.

Before starting the cast, Joan strips in slack until she has tension on the line, leaning forward and reaching out as far as she can. The line is started on its rearward journey by moving casting arm and body back so that the weight is shifted back to the rear foot, the right one (see Plate 61). Meanwhile, up comes the left hand, almost to the stripping guide, to grasp the line for the haul. Joan picks up the line from the water with a decisive lift, yanking down sharply into the haul as the line leaves the water (see Plate 62). At the finish of the pick-up, she turns her casting hand into the free-wrist position to enable her to toss that back cast up there where it belongs (see Plate 63). The haul, working in conjunction with the pick-up and lift into the high back cast, aids in speeding the line to its rearward destination.

As the line travels to the rear, Joan takes no chances. You will note that she turns her head to watch its progress. At the same time her casting hand turns to the free-wrist position. As the back cast nears completion she follows through with the rod tip almost to the two o'clock position.

Before starting the forward cast, Joan reaches up again, almost to the stripping guide, to grasp the line (see Plate

Plate 60. World's professional woman fly caster, Joan Salvato of Miami. Holder of many titles and one of the few casters (male or female) to defeat the late John Dieckman in competition, Joan is the scourge of the professional casting circuit.

Plate 61. Rod well extended for maximum arc, Joan Salvato begins a powerful back cast. Note that she leans well forward while her left hand starts the lift-off haul.

Plate 62. In full lift-off, Joan Salvato shows the power that can be generated in a small package. Her weight shifts to the rear and her haul is in midstage as she braces herself against the drag of 75 feet of line in the air.

Plate 63. Weight all the way back, Joan turns to watch her back cast in flight. Her left arm is moving toward full haul extension as she rides the cast rearward on follow-through.

Plate 64. Applying full power, Joan starts her weight shift forward with the cast. Her casting hand is now well over on the top of the rod grip, and her left hand has moved up to stop the back cast shoot preparatory to beginning the forward haul.

Plate 65. Driving the cast, Joan is now in full weight shift forward. Her left arm has reached peak extension on the forward haul just prior to "shoot" release. Note that the rod is nearly straight at this point, showing that her tremendous power comes from the middle rod rather than late tip action.

64). She starts the line forward first with movement of the arm and body, shifting weight gradually from right to left foot, but leaving the rod tip back near the two o'clock position. Next the rod tip starts forward, gradually accelerating. As she does this, once again the hand is shifted to place the thumb on top of the grip so that she can apply full power to the cast. As the rod speeds up, the forward haul goes into action, finishing as the rod tip reaches the point of release. Now the weight is completely on the left foot and Joan leans forward into the cast, putting all of her 115 pounds into the effort, her left hand and arm extended well to the rear at the completion of the haul (see Plate 65). Once the cast is completed at the point of release—aimed high so that she can take full advantage of every inch of "shoot"—Joan releases the line, and the line-handler feeds the slack up as she guides it to the stripping guide. The whole operation, beautifully timed and with faultless coordination, shows countless hours of practice. It is truly a lovely thing to watch.

Joan isn't satisfied with one back cast when trying for distance. She will false-cast until she has the absolute maximum of line in the air before turning loose the final cast. And with *every* cast, false cast or final cast, she executes a full haul, forward and back.

Of course, for everyday fishing the extreme motions that Joan goes through are not practical. You will recall the warning against shifting the weight either in a bass-bug boat, canoe, or bonefish skiff. In the first place, shifting the weight is dangerous; it also sends out warning wavelets or ripples. But modifications of her movements will add many feet to your cast when those feet are needed.

For example, use a modified haul to aid your pick-up. Instead of making your pick-up in the usual way, move your left hand up to grasp the line about next to the reel seat, with the casting arm fully extended. You can't reach any farther without shifting weight. Start the line by moving your arm and casting hand, *tilting the wrist slightly forward as you do*, so that the rod tip does not lose any of its arc of motion. Now, start your rod tip into the back cast, and as you execute the lift into the high back cast, haul the line down with your left hand sharply so that it passes your left hip.

As the line travels rearward, let some slack move out with it in the first part of the double shoot, allowing it to move through the ringed thumb and index finger of the left hand; that way you always have control of your line. As this rearward shoot moves out let the left hand ride up with it once more to the reel seat. This hand, as you know, checks the line at the completion of the back cast. Toss the back cast high and follow through with the rod tip to about the two o'clock position, with the casting arm extended up and back.

At the completion of the back cast, start the line forward by the forward motion of the hand and arm, *this time tilting the hand slightly back* in order to keep the rod tip in position. Execute the forward haul sharply, with the left hand slashing down and rearward past the left hip as you complete the forward cast. Performed properly, these modifications should add no less than 25 feet to what would have been a normal 60- or 70-foot cast.

You can't expect to go through this rather complicated set of motions without practice, a *lot* of practice. But if you will take the time to learn these motions and learn them thoroughly, you will find that the time and trouble involved in practice will pay off in that priceless bonus of extra feet when those vital feet are needed.

FLY-ROD EQUIPMENT:
REELS, LINES AND LEADERS

12

W EBSTER defines a reel as "a kind of small wind-lass for the butt end of a fishing rod, to wind up or let out line." Technically, that is what a reel is—a windlass to wind up or let out line—but it is far more. Today's reel does three things for the angler. It balances the rod; it carries, ready for instant use, the fly line and the necessary backing; and it plays an important part in the battle after a fish has been hooked.

Rod-and-Reel Balance

In the matter of rod-and-reel balance, theoretically the approximate ratio is 1½ to 1. In other words, the reel should weigh 1½ times the weight of the rod. Actually, this rule (first set up during the bamboo-rod era, long before glass rods were available) is a flexible one. Today's glass rods are lighter and more powerful than the equivalent in bamboo. Thus, rod-and-reel balance may be considered as a 2 to 1 ratio and still not be too far out of line.

Frankly, it has always seemed that the matter of rod-and-reel balance has been overstressed in its importance.

For example, consider the ratio of salt-water fly rods and reels. Here a good glass "flat rod" in 9½ feet weights 5¾ ounces. The #3 Fin-Nor reel that goes with this rod weighs 16 ounces, an even pound. Of course, this combination is completely out of gear with the accepted rod-and-reel ratio for balance. And when the outfit is held stationary in the hand, the weight of the reel seems to be well out of proportion. But don't forget—this "flat rod" is a powerhouse, a tremendously strong rod. Once it is put to work, handling a goodly length of forward-taper line, the rod and reel seem to balance perfectly. Actually, rod-and-reel balance can be reduced to a matter of comfortable "feel" when casting and in actual use.

For example, this same #3 Fin-Nor reel was fixed to a bamboo Winston bonefish rod, the same length as the glass flat rod—9½ feet—and weighing approximately 6 ounces. This rod does not begin to have the power of the glass flat rod and cannot handle the same length of line. In this combination the reel is a complete misfit and overbalances the rod.

In bamboo trout rods, the reels attached, the balancing point should be 1½ or 2 inches above the top of the cork grip. Not so with glass rods. A light glass trout rod, 4¼ ounces, 8 feet long, feels quite comfortable with a Heddon reel weighing 7 ounces—almost a 2-to-1 ratio. By the same token, this same reel will overbalance a bamboo rod of 8 feet, 5⅛ ounces. Actually, if there is a hard-and-fast rule of rod balance, it has yet to come to our attention. Boiling it all down, it is entirely a matter of comfortable casting. There are far too many intangibles (weight of fittings, weight of reel seat, action distribution, etc.) to attempt to set down a definite rule.

Selecting a Reel

There are many things in the construction of a fly reel which go to make a good or bad reel. Consider the line guide through which the line passes as it is spooled onto the reel drum or arbor. A square line guide, wide enough to enable the user to spool on the line evenly from side plate to side plate, is a good line guide. Conversely, a round line guide inescapably piles up the line on the center of the drum. This means that the line capacity of the reel is reduced appreciably. Also, turns of line from the top of the pile-up tend to fall off and overlap, and this, in turn, leads to tangles and over-runs when line is paid out. Avoid the round line guides; they are a nuisance.

One of the best reels for all-round trout fishing is Garcia's Beaudex. It is sturdily built, has plenty of line capacity, and the click is adjustable and nonoscillating. On the older Beaudex there was a square line guide fastened to a pillar or space bar by a machine screw. This could be attached to either side of the reel for right-handed or left-handed reeling. The more recent Beaudex reels have a fitted line guide made of heavy steel wire with a half-round bend over which the line must pass (see Plate 66). In effect, it is a round line guide. After half an hour of fooling with this miserable makeshift, it was ripped off and flung halfway across the East Branch of the Delaware River. Now the space bar or pillar, suitably rounded off with file and emery paper, serves as a line guide.

In one of the big trout rivers of central Pennsylvania there are some monster brown trout that seem to specialize in feeding on small flies—tiny things, size 16 and 18. Naturally, a heavy leader point attached to one of the small artificial counterparts stands out like a cable. In order to induce these big fish to take, leader points of not more than 6X must be used. For the use of 6X points, it follows that a reel with a soft click is indicated. The best that has appeared so far is the Heddon Imperial. Although Heddon has discontinued this reel, you can still find them in the tackleshops. A big trout simply cannot break a 6X point against the soft click of this reel.

The line capacity of a reel is an important item. Even on small trout reels, a certain amount of backing is advisable. (Backing, if you happen not to be familiar with the term, is an underwrap of fairly fine line that is wound on the reel drum or arbor between the drum and the casting line.) True, you don't need this backing often when you are fishing small streams, but when you do happen to hook a large fish, that same backing can be vastly important. Even for small streams and light rods, a reel with a drum whose side plates measure not less than 2⅞ inches is indicated. The Hardy Lightweight is an excellent example of this type of reel. Another is the Ted Williams fly reel that is made for Sears Roebuck & Company by the Bronson Company.

For bass-bug fishing, you are of course using a big rod (at least, you should be). This means that a fairly large reel should be used. Out of the many that have been tried, perhaps the 1498 Pflueger Medalist is the most practical (see Plate 67). This reel is just about right in weight for balancing a bass-bug rod. In addition, its large drum provides ample space for backing and casting line. The wide diameter of the drum, when filled to capacity, provides a fast recovery of line. Each turn of a filled spool brings in approximately 9 inches of line, which gives it just about the fastest line recovery of any fly reel on the market. This reel has a fairly satisfactory drag, enough for the job in hand. It does tend to oscillate if not set up fairly tight, but it is strong enough to check the run of a heavy bass. A 6-pound smallmouth can give a good account of himself in a scrap, but the Medalist will stop him on a sustained run inside of 50 yards.

Reels for salmon fishing and salt-water fishing are something else again. Here you have three vital factors to consider—line capacity, stoutness of drag, and strength of spool or drum.

It is a rare thing for a game fish—*any* game fish—to make a sustained run of more than 200 yards against the drag of any reasonably good reel. To be sure, you hear tales of big game fish going off with 200 and 300 yards of fly line and backing, stripping line right down to the reel drums. As a matter of fact, we have not only seen it happen but have had it happen to us. There is little that can be done when a big fish decides to walk off with your gear, except to apply all the pressure the tackle will bear and pray that he stops before the critical point is reached. Moreover, there is no way to provide effective measures against such a contingency. When it happens, it happens—and that's that. You can only rerig with the spare reel and hope it does not happen again.

The good salmon and salt-water reels have a line capacity of around 300 yards, using 18-pound nylon backing and the usual 120 feet of fly line. A reel that holds more line than that is apt to be too cumbersome for comfortable everyday use.

The factor that decides whether a reel for salmon fishing or salt-water fishing is a good reel or a bad reel is the quality of the drag. Most tournament regulations limit the strength of the leader point to 12-pounds break test. Thus, a reel which has a drag that can be set at 6 or 8 pounds is

←

Plate 66.   One of the best of the middle-priced imports is this Beaudex fly reel handled by Garcia. It possesses the most even drag of any dry-fly reel used in this country today. The Beaudex is a dependable, solid investment.

→

Plate 67.   Leading the medium-priced field, the 1498 Pflueger Medalist is one of the more popular light-tackle bass-bug and salt-water reels. Constructed of anodized alloy, this reel is virtually corrosionproof. It also boasts the most rapid retrieve in salt-water fly tackle, allowing the angler nearly 9 inches per reel handle turn.

Plate 68.   Precision-crafted like a fine watch, the Fin-Nor salmon and salt-water fly reels lead the field in quality, with the widest drag flange constructed in any fly reel today. These reels can generate up to 14 pounds of nonoscillating full drag pressure.

quite adequate. Remember, the drag on a reel is usually set when the reel is filled to capacity with line. Thus, the distance from the center of the reel drum to the top edge of the line on the reel can be considered as the lever which pulls against the drag. As the line is paid out, this lever is shortened. When half the line is taken from the spool, this lever is reduced by one half. In accordance with the laws of physics, if the length of the lever is reduced to one half, the amount of force needed to turn the reel against the drag is doubled. Thus a 6-pound drag on a full reel drum means a 12-pound drag when the line is half run off the reel. Add to this the friction of the line passing through the water and the guides of your rod, and you will find that a 6-pound drag soon reaches the danger point as the diameter of the line on the reel is reduced.

But don't confuse starting tension with tension while the reel is spinning. Some drags may very well require a 6-pound pull to set the reel drum in motion. But once the reel is in motion, the drag is reduced to as little as 1 or 2 pounds. Steer clear of these drags. They are known as oscillating drags and can cause all sorts of trouble. Buy a reel with a smooth, steady drag that starts at the set strength and *stays* there, no matter what the fish decides to do.

There are two reels for salmon and salt-water fishing which stand the drag test very well—the Zwarg and the Fin-Nor. The Zwarg is equipped with a perimeter drag —two leather pads which impinge against the side of the drum plate, supported by a phosphor bronze spring, the tension of which can be increased. This drag can be set up to 4 or 5 pounds—plenty for a 12-pound leader point. It seems to last well under hard usage, and by and large is quite satisfactory.

The Fin-Nor drag is a multiple-disc affair built around the center post (see Plate 68). It is smooth, and equally important, constant. Starting tension and running tension are the same. It is a fine piece of mechanism.

The drags on both of these reels operate in only one direction—when the line is going out. When line is being recovered, you do not wind against drag tension.

But there are other considerations about these two reels. The Zwarg design gives firm support to both ends of the center post. You can drop these reels and do very little damage, as the center post is solidly anchored. The Fin-Nor design is very bad in this respect. The center post is of narrow diameter, much too small, and is supported by a single, inadequate anchorage in the back of the reel frame. The least jolt or jar will knock this post out of line. Even the sudden tug of a big fish will pull the center post sufficiently out of line to cause the side plate of the drum to lock against the reel frame. This lamentable defect has caused the loss of many a fish that would certainly have been of record poundage. Therefore, while trying to be fair to both manufacturers, in our opinion the Zwarg will give more dependable service over the years.

Incidentally, Zwarg not only makes single-action reels, but also multipliers geared to a 2½-to-1 ratio. You can't tell a single-action from a multiplier just by looking at it, for the two appear identical. A multiplier such as Zwarg's 2½-to-1 model allows the angler to gain 2½ turns of the reel spool for every revolution of the reel handle. They are great laborsavers, but not allowed in most tournaments. Also, the Zwarg has a unique line guide in the form of a revolving space bar or pillar, one on each side. This feature reduces line wear considerably.

One thing in a salt-water reel that should be avoided at

all costs is an insecurely assembled drum. When you re-
cover line against a big fish, you are winding that line
under tension. Nylon backing has a certain amount of
elasticity. Thus when you wind on turn after turn of elastic
line, internal stresses are set up inside the coils of line on
the drum. With an improperly designed reel drum, it is
not uncommon to have that drum "explode." This locks
the mechanism and away goes a good fish. You won't have
any trouble with the Zwarg or the Fin-Nor in this respect,
as you will with some of the other reels on the market.

Fly-Casting Lines

It took the rope and twine manufacturers of the world
a long, long time to learn how to make satisfactory fly-
casting lines. In Izaak Walton's day, anglers braided their
own lines out of horsehair—the long hairs from the horse's
tail. As late as 1890 or so, about the best that a man could
get in the average sporting-goods store in the way of a
fly-casting line was a heavy braided line of cotton, evidently "weighted" or sized to give it some body. Then,
in the early nineteen hundreds, some genius developed
"enameled lines." At least these were a big improvement
on anything then available, but they were not good. They
were also called, by the irreverent, "linoleum lines." A
reel coil was developed that made them act like a watch
spring, but once "broken in," they would slide through the
guides, and they had enough backbone to cast fairly well.

A letter dated January 2, 1947, from a famous British
angler, the late G. E. M. Skues of London, throws an interesting sidelight on early line manufacture. The following
is, in part, what he had to say on the subject:

"The earliest makers of a tapered fly casting line were
the Manchester Cotton Twine Spinning Company of Man-

chester, England, and Eaton & Deller of Crooked Lane, London. The Manchester line was not woven but was a twisted or laid line composed of silk and cotton or line, not oil-dressed but quite hard and durable. The Eaton & Deller line was a tapered, silk-woven line, oil-dressed much as our lines are today.

"It is not clear which of these companies was first in the field with the tapered line, but the two introductions were so closely simultaneous that it is only fair to give credit to both companies. These lines were brought out during the early eighties.

"After Deller's death, Mr. Halford consulted a surgical-instrument maker named Hawksby, a distinguished angler who considerably improved the details of line dressing. In fact, he was said to have made a definitely better job of it than any tackle manufacturer. Halford insisted on the line being woven solid—not hollow. Also, that the taper at each end, from thickest to finest, should be five yards as against Deller's six yards.

"Shortly thereafter Mr. Walter D. Coggeshell of this country [England] turned out tapered lines that were dressed with a combination of oil and varnish. These are the best lines that I ever saw or heard of. This was in the late nineties. In 1902, Mr. Coggeshell presented me with one of his lines which stood the test of time for over thirty years of hard wear."

It wasn't long before the American linemakers followed suit with braided silk lines, tapered at each end and oil-dressed. The process, roughly, consisted of stretching the braided lines between pegs in a line loft and applying coat after coat of linseed oil, each coat being allowed to dry before the next one was applied. Some companies used a "dryer" in the oil to hasten the operation. Others mixed in a small amount of varnish. When enough coats were applied to cover the braid completely, the line was polished to a high gloss.

This finish was comparatively soft and wore away rather quickly, exposing the braid. Also, the finish would oxidize and become "tacky." This condition could be corrected, temporarily, by soaking the line in limewater. Then the finish could be reinforced by the application of a half-and-half mixture of linseed oil and spar varnish. But these repairs were a nuisance. The best thing to do when a line became tacky, was to throw it away and buy a new one.

Although the oil dressings of our fly lines gradually improved over the years, it was a boon to anglers when plastic finishes found their way into line manufacture. Today our nylon and dacron braids, with modern plastic finishes, are the fly-fisherman's joy and delight. These finishes take a high polish so that they shoot well. Impregnation of the finish with air bubbles renders the floating lines actually sinkproof. Conversely, the dacron lines sink readily and are ideal for underwater fishing with wet flies, streamers and sinking lures.

Size Designations for Lines

Many years ago line sizes were set up alphabetically, as follows:

Size	Diameter
A	.060″
B	.055″
C	.050″
D	.045″
E	.040″
F	.035″
G	.030″
H	.025″
I	.020″

In the double A and triple A sizes, the diameter went up in proportion, five thousandths of an inch per size.

Fly lines are put out in various braidings. The lines of one continuous diameter, from one end to the other, are known as "level lines." Level lines which taper at one end are called "single tapers." Those with tapers at each end, with a continuous diameter through the middle part of the line, are called "double tapers." The more recent multiple tapers are known variously as "torpedo head," "forward taper," "weight-forward tapers," "rocket tapers" and so on. Generally these lines are of three diameters—a fairly short front taper terminating in a small diameter; then a heavy "belly" portion of large diameter; this tapers down into a level "running line" which continues uniform to the end which is fastened to the reel or backing.

Level lines are designated by only one size letter, showing the approximate diameter. Single tapers have two-letter designations. For example—HD. This means that the diameter at the end of the taper is .025 inch, while the remainder of the line, back from the completion of the taper, has a diameter of .045 inch. The multiple tapers are designated by three letters. For example—GAF. This means that the forward end of the taper at the end of the line has a diameter of .030 inch; the heavy section or "belly" has a diameter of .060 inch; and the running line, between the belly and the reel end, has a diameter of .035 inch.

This method of size designation was fine as long as manufacturing procedures were more or less standardized —braided silk with linseed-oil finish. Specific gravities of lines varied but little in those days. With the advent of the synthetics—nylon, dacron, etc.— the line picture began to change rapidly. While size A still indicated a diameter of .060 inch the *weight* of a line of that diameter could show wide variation. Thus, a rod which could handle a GBF braided silk line comfortably could very well step up to a GAF or a GA-AF line in braided nylon with the air-impregnated finish. Alphabetical line sizes ceased to mean very much. Then, too, the manufacturers did not standardize on the length of the belly in a three-diameter line. You would find the heavy section anywhere from 18 to 30 feet in length. This of course meant a wide variation in line load on the rod when the line was used in actual casting.

Recognizing this fact, a committee was formed from representatives of the line companies, the National Association of Angling and Casting Clubs, and the International Federation of Casters, the purpose of which was to do something about line-size designations which would tell an angler, at a glance, just what he was buying. The committee decided on the following system of standards.

To determine the weight of a line, only the front 30 feet are considered—that is, from the *end of the forward taper,* back 30 feet. This weight is given in grains. (A grain is a unit of weight derived arbitrarily from the weight of a grain of wheat—7,000 grains constitute a pound avoirdupois.) Admittedly, the weight designations are somewhat complicated. Let's see if we can't simplify matters a bit.

First, weights are indicated by code numbers, as shown on page 168.

The weight, as stated, is given in grains. Since it is difficult to manufacture lines to exact tolerances, there may be slight variations in material weights, diameters, etc. The range provides for this contingency, indicating an allowable tolerance variation schedule of 6 to 12 grains on either side of the true code weight, according to the size of the line.

Code No.	Weight in grains	Range
1	60	54-66
2	80	74-86
3	100	94-106
4	120	114-126
5	140	134-146
6	160	152-168
7	185	177-193
8	210	202-218
9	240	230-250
10	280	270-290
11	330	318-342
12	380	368-392

In addition, identification symbols were set up, as follows:

L   — Level
S   — Sinking Line
ST — Single Taper
DT — Double Taper
F   — Floating Line
I   — Intermediate, floating or sinking
WF — Weight Forward Taper

Thus, L5F means a level floating line with approximately 140 grains of weight in the front 30 feet.

WF9F would mean a weight-forward line—bug or rocket taper—floating variety, the weight of the front 30 feet being 240 grains.

For those who will not take the trouble to find out what the new designations mean, the line manufacturers also include the old alphabetical designations. So if you see the double designations on the box of a new line—GAF-WF9F—you have the whole story.

As a rule, double-taper lines come in 90-foot lengths. The three-diameter lines usually are from 110 to 120 feet long.

Some of the line companies are now turning out "casting heads" for fly fishermen who like to get plenty of distance without too much effort. These seem to vary somewhat with the manufacturer, but most of them are around 40 feet long, tapered at one end in the orthodox fly-casting taper. At the other end, the diameters taper slightly so that the casting head can be whipped onto nylon mono-filament, with which the reel can be filled. Casting heads are fine for those who like them. For comfortable fishing, the regular double-taper or three-diameter seems to be better.

Tournament casters use casting heads almost to the complete exclusion of orthodox lines. These are complicated affairs, built pretty much according to the ideas of the caster in question. For example, here are the specifications of the casting head that John Salvato uses for distance casting:

.040″	.045″	.050″	.055″	.060″	.065″	.070″	.075″	.060″	.050″	.040″
1½′	2′	3′	7′	8′	10′	8′	10′	2′	1½′	1½′

Front   Rear

Fifty-four and one-half feet with 11 diameters, all braided into one casting head—a complicated job of line braiding; also, quite expensive. Some of the tournament casters make their own casting heads, splicing the various diameters together. This method, while less expensive, makes for a fairly rough line with sharp variations in diameter at the splices. The braided job, such as Joan uses, is more satisfactory.

Selecting a Line to Fit a Rod

Just as rod-and-reel balance is an extremely flexible matter, so is the job of finding a line that is best suited to a rod. Some manufacturers flatly state that a certain fly rod takes a definite line size. Nothing could be further from the truth. No two fly rods have exactly the same weight and the same length, yet even if they are almost identical, one may take an HCH line while the other will drop back two full sizes to an HEH.

After experimenting for a great many years with the task of matching lines to rods, the inevitable conclusion has been that the only way to do this satisfactorily is by the time-tested method of trial and error. To be sure, not very many anglers have a battery of lines and reels for test purposes, but most men have several friends who have two or three line-and-reel combinations. The best thing to do is to impose on their good nature and try out several lines on a new rod before deciding what line to buy. In this way you can get *exactly* the right line and not an approximation.

One last caution about lines—for light rods and trout fishing, better stick to orthodox double tapers. For this type of fishing, where you will need a complete repertoire of special casts, the double taper gives by far the best performance. Three-diameter lines tend to turn over too fast for trout fishing, making it difficult to drop a fly lightly to the surface or to throw such casts as the negative curve, etc.

Conversely, for casting bass bug and salmon fly (wet or streamer fly) the three-diameter is surely indicated, just as it is in salt-water fly fishing. Your choice of floating or sinking lines will naturally depend upon the type of fishing that you happen to be doing.

Backing

As explained earlier, it is wise to use backing on *every* reel, regardless of size. Just about any reel that you buy will fail to have its drum filled to capacity by the fly line alone. For ease of line handling and speed of line recovery, a reel drum should be completely filled with line.

Time was when we had to depend on silk or linen braided line for backing. This was not too satisfactory, since these two materials tend to deteriorate with time. Repeated wettings and dryings will rot them, and thus tensile strength is reduced. Not infrequently, this reduction of breaking strength can result in the complete loss of line and backing when a heavy fish takes out line down to the reel drum. Now that we have nylon and dacron braided lines for backing, this loss in tensile strength has been eliminated, since these materials are not affected by water.

It is always wise to use backing that is several pounds stronger than your leader point. For example, if you are using a 12-pound leader point, your backing certainly should test at from 16 pounds to 18 pounds.

All of the line manufacturers turn out braided nylon and dacron lines. Any of the casting lines or squidding lines make good backing, always provided the pound test is strong enough. Nylon and dacron, impervious to the effects of water, need little or no care. Some anglers use monofilament for backing, but this is not nearly as satisfactory as a soft braided casting or squidding line in nylon or dacron.

Winding on the exact amount of line and backing to fill a reel spool to capacity is something of a job. To eliminate guesswork and needless waste of braided backing, wind the casting line onto the reel drum first. Then wind on backing until the reel is full. By doing this, it is possible to cut the backing to exact size, with no loss. Next, either transfer the backing to another reel, a line winder, or some convenient object such as a large book. This done, coil the fly line on the floor or on the couch and spool on your backing, taking care that the winds are put on evenly, back and forth across the drum, from one side plate to the other.

The casting line can be attached to the backing in two ways. The two ends can be whipped together with solid wraps of silk or nylon thread and then varnished. This method assures that little or no tensile strength is lost at the juncture. The more flexible and perhaps easier way is to whip a small loop into the end of the fly line, using silk or nylon thread, and varnish the wrap when it is completed. Then tie a large loop, about 6 inches long, in the end of the backing, using a bowline or the knot that is used at the top of a leader. Slip this loop through the small loop at the end of the fly line; then pass the big loop in the backing over the reel and pull the two loops together so that they form, in effect, a square knot. By using 18-pound backing for a leader point of 12 pounds, you allow enough factor of safety to insure against any possible loss of tensile strength at the knot in the backing. With this method, it is a simple matter to change lines on your reel without going through all the bother of whipping the two ends together and then varnishing.

Care of Lines

It is not a good plan to leave lines on the reels from one season to the next. While present-day finishes stand up infinitely better than the old linseed-oil finishes, they are not indestructible. When the fishing season is over, it is better to coil your lines loosely in cardboard boxes. Get boxes large enough to hold both a reel and a line in fairly large, loose coils. Then store the boxes in a cool, dry place until the following season.

The importance of line dressing has been greatly diminished since the introduction of the floating lines. There was a time when a coat of line dressing was essential to comfortable dry-fly fishing. Now your line will float, dressing or no dressing. Some of the line companies enclose in the boxes with the new lines small tins of what they call "line cleaner." Actually this is a line dressing, but it does serve to clean your line as well as to keep it floating, high and dry. It is a good plan to go over a line now and then with line cleaner on a soft cloth.

Always be careful to keep your line free of sand or grit. Line dressing will pick up particles of sand. Then when the line passes through the guides of your rod, the effect is much like passing a piece of fine emery paper through those guides. The abrasion wears down both the guides and the line finish. In boats, where slack line is coiled on the floor or the forward deck, the area should always be sponged or brushed clean of sand, dirt, etc., as should the soles of the angler's shoes.

While it is advisable to dry lines after use, it is not really necessary, since finishes and nylon and dacron backing are not affected by water to any great extent. In salt-water fishing, it is a good idea to wipe a line dry after using. Salt crystals act as an abrasive, just as sand does, and your lines will keep their slick finishes longer if they are kept clean.

Leaders

When leaders were made of silk-worm gut, every angler had a leader problem. In those days leaders were kept moist between the felt pads of leader boxes. There was always trouble keeping leaders usable and strong. Mildew in leader pads—a common occurrence—could ruin leaders overnight. Repeated wetting and drying weakened silk-worm gut. Even sunlight would spoil leaders; they had to be stored in a cool, dark, dry place.

When nylon was first introduced as leader material, it was not too satisfactory. The first nylon leader strands were highly susceptible to temperature changes. As long as water temperatures were in the sixties or over, nylon functioned quite well. But in the early spring, when water temperatures were down in the high thirties and forties, nylon became brittle. Leaders would break, for no evident reason, right in the center of a strand, nowhere near the knots. They were every bit as big a headache as gut leaders.

Gradually, however, the quality of nylon was improved. Today it is excellent leader material, although not all nylon is of the same quality. Also, there are several other synthetic monofilaments on the market which are just about as good. The plastic manufacturers are learning a great deal about the making of leader material. In addition, monofilament is now used on both quadruple-multiplier casting reels and spinning reels, in preference to orthodox braided casting lines.

With this variety of uses and demands, the linemakers are doing all sorts of things with monofilament, the main object being to soften the material and to take out the "stretch" or elasticity to provide for sure hooking.

Naturally, the soft monofilament is not good for fly-casting leaders. One of the outstanding advantages of silkworm gut is its hardness and comparative inflexibility. At the end of a cast, you want a leader that has some spring and backbone so that it will turn over and not collapse into a "bird's nest." Gut will do this for you; soft monofilament will not. So when you are buying coils of monofilament for tying your own leaders, make sure that you are getting hard, stiff material that has some body and snap to it.

Some of the newer monofilaments have tensile strengths which were unheard of in silkworm gut. For example, one of them comes in 6X and 7X strands (so labeled on the package) which will pull unbelievable poundage. The 6X strands, which calibrate five-thousands of an inch, actually have a break test of 1.9 pounds. The 7X strands, slightly over four thousandths of an inch in diameter, will pull ¾ of a pound. Going up the scale, the 2X strands—nine-thousandths of an inch in diameter—break at slightly under 5 pounds. But there is a catch to all this. The material is extremely soft and nonresilient and is of little use in fly-rod leaders. About the only way to use these strong, fine strands as terminal tackle is to tie on a strand of not more than 18 inches at the end of a good nylon casting leader. For fishing small flies—16, 18 and 20—for leader-shy trout, the stuff is ideal, but it is useless for the construction of entire leaders.

A fly-casting leader, in order to handle well and turn over your fly at the completion of a cast, should be tapered. Where the leader is fastened to the line, the size of the leader material should be somewhere near that of the end of the line. Then it should taper down to the desired leader size to be fastened to your fly or lure. This tapering serves to dissipate the force of the cast as the leader turns over, allowing the fly to reach the surface lightly. A level leader turns over much too fast for the delicate job of dry-fly fishing.

By and large, the leaders that are ready-tied and nicely packaged at the sporting-goods stores aren't worth using. Most of the ready-made leaders are far too light through the top strands and are badly tapered. By far the best way to get satisfactory leaders is to tie them yourself. Tying leaders is not a difficult job. Anyone with normal manual dexterity can tie up a leader. There are only two knots to learn—the leader loop and the barrel knot or blood knot—and these are easily mastered. You will find them in the illustration sketches of angler's knots (Plate 69).

Leader Tapers

For trout fishing, particularly dry-fly fishing, we like what we call the "steep-taper" leader. The top strand of this leader should be fairly close in size to the end of the front taper of your line in order to dissipate the force of the cast evenly through the turnover. By "size" is meant "comparative flexibility" not "comparative diameters." Thus, for use with an HCH, HDH or HEH line (the usual trout lines), the top strand should be seventeen thousandths of an inch in diameter. The steep-taper trout leader should be put together as follows:

Diameter	.017″	.015″	.013″	.011″	.009″	.007″	.006″
Length of Strand in Inches	12″	12″	33″	12″	12″	12″	18″

This works out to a leader of approximately 9 feet, 3 inches in length, tapered to 5X. If you wish to cut back to 4X, eliminate the .006-inch strand and lengthen the .007-inch strand to 18 inches. This will give you an 8-foot 3-inch leader, tapered to 4X.

For wet-fly leaders, many anglers like to fish nothing finer than 3X. This same leader can be cut back two strands and then a strand of 3X (.008-inch) can be added. If you prefer 2X, cut back the first two strands and then add a couple of feet of 2X (.009-inch) material. This taper is quite flexible in its uses and can easily be adapted to just about any style of trout fishing by simply substituting the indicated strands in the two or three finer diameters.

Sometimes, when fishing large streams for line-shy and leader-shy trout, it is both advisable and expedient to lengthen your leader to 12 feet. You can use the same taper specifications as shown above, except that you add 18 inches to the top strand of .017 inch and 18 inches to the second strand of .015 inch. Most anglers, as a matter of convenience, carry a couple of 12-foot leaders. An easier way, however, is to have in your leader pack a "leader extension." This consists, simply, of 3 feet of .017-inch nylon monofilament, preferably tied in two strands, and with a loop at each end. Then when a 12-foot leader is

ANGLER'S KNOTS

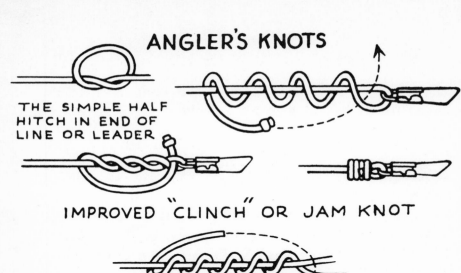

THE SIMPLE HALF HITCH IN END OF LINE OR LEADER

IMPROVED "CLINCH" OR JAM KNOT

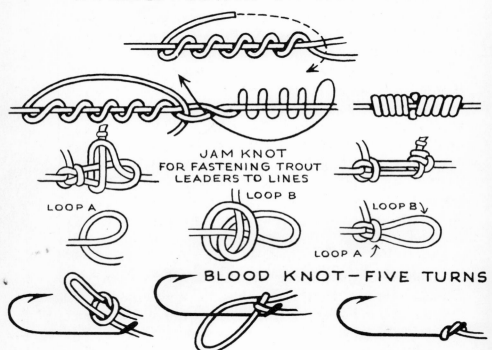

JAM KNOT FOR FASTENING TROUT LEADERS TO LINES

LOOP A   LOOP B   LOOP B

LOOP A

BLOOD KNOT—FIVE TURNS

TURLE KNOT FOR TROUT FLIES, BASS FLIES & BUGS ETC

FIG. EIGHT KNOT FOR SALMON FLIES

FOR TYING ENDS OF LINE OR LEADER OF DIFFERENT DIAMETERS

Plate 69

indicated, all you need to do is to loop in the leader extension between the line and the leader you are using.

Fastening a Leader to a Line

For fastening a leader to a line, some men like to have a loop whipped in at the end of the line. That's all right for bass-bug, salmon-fly or salt-water fishing. But for trout fishing, where change of leaders is apt to be a frequent operation, the jam knot is preferable. This simple knot, with a simple overhand knot tied into the line end, can be loosened easily to permit change of leaders.

No matter what method you use to fasten line to leader, remember that the end of your line proper—just where it joins either the loop or the jam knot—is subject to quite a lot of bending. Thus the fibers of the line grow tired and the tensile strength is cut down, often to the danger point. Test this spot frequently and renew the loop or cut back the knot area when indicated. Nothing can be more exasperating than needless failure of terminal tackle.

Leader Sizes and Diameters

During the latter part of the silkworm-gut era, there was some confusion in leader diameters and the size labels. At that time, 4X was supposed to calibrate .006 inch. Then some of the leader-supply houses began to get a little careless. A packaged leader would be labeled NINE FEET, TAPERED TO 4x. Investigation would show that the leader point actually calibrated .007 inch instead of the indicated .006 inch. The gullible angler who did not own a micrometer or a leader gauge would give the manufacturer credit for making leaders of extra-strong material, not knowing that he was fishing with a leader point that was one size heavier than advertised.

When synthetic leaders came on the market, the companies finally got together and agreed to make leader diameters and sizes uniform. Starting with the smaller diameters, the scale today looks like this:

Size	Diameter in thousandths of an inch
5X	.006″
4X	.007″
3X	.008″
2X	.009″
1X	.010″
0X	.011″

From 0X, up through the heavier diameters, monofilament is graded by pound-test designations. These are not too trustworthy. Some of the factories actually do have the forethought to include both pound-test figures and diameters in thousandths of an inch on the cards on which the coils are mounted. But most of them do not. It is best to have your own micrometer or leader gauge and do your own calibrating when you are buying leader material.

As you compare the designations on the leader cards of the various manufacturers, you will find a pronounced lack of uniformity in pound-test figures and diameters. For example, the Du Pont Company formerly listed 12-pound test at a flat nineteen thousandths. Not so today. Now monofilament is not distributed just as it comes from the extrusion machines. All sorts of things are done to it, such as the "hot stretch" process which takes much of the elasticity from the finished material. These processes inevitably reduce diameters. Unfortunately, however, they do not do so uniformly. Evidently, monofilament reacts variously to these processes with the result that you must deal in averages.

Consider this schedule which was received from the Du Pont Company, listing specifications for the stiff monofilament, made to be used in fly-casting leaders:

Diameters in thousandths of an inch	Break test in pounds Minimum	Average
.008″	3.5	3.7
.009″	4.0	4.5
.010″	4.5	5.5
.011″	5.2	6.2
.012″	6.2	7.4
.013″	7.2	8.7
.014″	8.1	9.7
.015″	9.0	11.5
.017″	11.7	14.5
.019″	14.6	18.0
.021″	17.6	21.7
.023″	21.0	26.0

Obviously, the only safe way to indicate monofilament strengths and diameters on a monofilament card would be to give the *minimum* break test per diameter. *Average* figures frequently would fall short of the mark. You will recall that 12-pound test formerly was listed at .019 inch. Take a look at the chart above; .019 inch here has a minimum break test of 14.6 and an average of 18 pounds.

The whole business is confusing and it is likely to become even more so until the makers find a way to standardize.

Many companies are now putting out tapered leaders in continuous, knotless strands. These leaders are of uniform taper. Frankly, the tied-up leaders of the steep-taper pattern give better casting performance. The knots do offer some water resistance when the leaders are picked up for the back cast, making the throwing of a high back cast somewhat easier. As has been said earlier, you will find it more satisfactory to tie your own leaders. That way you can get exactly what you want instead of having to use what the manufacturer thinks you should have.

Admittedly, what with lines, leaders and reels, glass and bamboo rods, and so on, fly fishing today is a complex business when compared with what is was 25 or 50 years ago. But, after all, fishing itself is a complicated sport. No one man can learn in a lifetime all there is to know about fishing. Count that day lost on lake or stream whose close has not brought with it some new and useful item of fishing knowledge. Complicated? Of course it's complicated. Were this not true, fishing would lose much of its charm.

ACKNOWLEDGMENTS

In writing a book, particularly one dealing with a technical subject, the author or authors must seek help in the accumulation of exact data. No one man, or two men, can possibly have all necessary information at the fingertips. And this is especially true about fishing. There is a tremendous amount of technical data related to fishing, any sort of fishing, and this includes fly casting.

Thus, we are indebted to many people who extended a helping hand in the preparation of this book. Arthur Mills of William Mills & Son gave us valuable material on the history of fly rods. Homer Circle, a busy vice-president of James Heddon's Sons, took time out from his many affairs to go into the factory and take pictures of the various steps in assembling a glass rod blank. Dick Jennings of the Cortland Line Company not only brought us up to date on the intricacies of listing fly-line sizes; he also sent us lines of the right color and taper to help us in our photographic work.

Doug Merrick of the Winston Rod Company sent us rods and valuable information on manufacturing methods. Dick Wolff of the Garcia Company not only sent us needed information but also loaned us Joan Salvato to pose for some of the casting pictures. And Joan, a busy housewife, took two days off from her duties and came down to the Florida Keys to do those pictures for us.

Thomas F. Bubin of the Shakespeare Company gave us much exact data on the early stages of glass-rod manufacture. John Pflueger of the Enterprise Manufacturing Company brought us up to date on bass-bug reels. Tycoon

Fin-Nor sent us photographs. And James D. Barhydt of E. I. Du Pont de Nemours & Company went to considerable trouble to dig up accurate data on breaking strengths of nylon monofilament.

And last, but not least by any means, Mrs. Richard Alden Knight—Jacqueline, or Pody as she is known professionally —took the action photographs. And what a job she did —not a retouched photograph in the entire lot.

To all of these good people and to many more who helped in one way or another, we wish to express our sincere gratitude and thanks.

INDEX

INDEX

187